What Evangeline Adams Knew

A Book of Astrological Charts and Techniques

Karen Christino

Stella Mira Books

Published by Stella Mira Books
P.O. Box 02-3095
Brooklyn, NY 11202
StellaMiraBooks@cs.com

Library of Congress Cataloging-in-Publication Data
Christino, Karen A.
    What Evangeline Adams knew: A book of astrological charts and techniques /
Karen A. Christino

    Includes bibliographical references and index.
    ISBN 10: 0-9725117-0-9   ISBN 13: 978-0-9725117-0-4
    1. Astrology. 2. Horoscopes.   I. Title.
133.54   2003104429

Cover design by Piero Galluzzo   Cover art by author

Printed in the United States of America

10 9 8 7 6 5 4 3 2

Contents

List of Horoscope Charts

For the teachers who in person and in print have helped shape my thinking: Al H. Morrison, Robert Zoller, Father Laurence L. Cassidy, Anthony Aveni, Zoltan Mason and Renée Randolph.

Acknowledgments

Research for this project was supported by a grant from the New York City chapter of the National Council for Geocosmic Research.

Some of the material in this book was originally published in different forms in *American Astrology, The Astrologers' Newsletter, Considerations, Fate, Mercury Hour*, NCGR's *Geocosmic, Journal* and *memberletter, The Traditional Astrologer*, and in "The Astrological Techniques of Evangeline Adams," a research paper written for the New York NCGR.

My gratitude and appreciation to Edward L. Dearborn for original material as well as his support over the years; Noel Tyl for his suggestions on the manuscript; Judith Werner for her editing expertise and advice; Lina Accurso for her feedback and unfailing enthusiasm; and to Diane L. Cramer for her proofreading and computer skills.

Many thanks to Marina Agassiz, Bill Breeze, Nick Campion, Lee Chapman, Don Christino, Edith Custer, Rabbi Joel C. Dobin, Ronnie Gale Dreyer, Larry Ely, Meira Epstein, Ken Gillman, Jim Haynes, Susan Luck Hooks, Deborah Houlding, Ken Irving, Mary E. Jarvis, Ken Kimball, Adam Kraar, Michael Lutin, John Marchesella, Maurice McCann, Frances McEvoy, Roxana Muise, Ann E. Parker, Nona Gwynn Press, Lois Rodden, Bruce Scofield, Joanna Shannon, Kaye Shinker, Joseph Silveira deMello, Georgia Stathis, Edwin Steinbrecher, Pat Taglilatelo, Lorraine Welsh, Judith Werner, Leigh Westin, Bonnie Wilson and Norman Winski.

Introduction

For over a century, people have been trying to discover Evangeline Adams' astrological secrets. She, herself, at times took the stance that she was privy to mysterious and occult knowledge to which others had no access; astrological expertise was certainly a rare commodity in her day. So it should be satisfying for all contemporary astrologers to learn that Adams was just a good, solid astrologer, not especially skilled either technically or theoretically. Yet she knew her astrology well and believed in herself and her craft. She saw about eight clients a day (in later years 25 a week). Such a great amount of feedback from clients can only have sharpened her skills, and she always remained fascinated with astrology.

This book is intended as a practicing astrologer's handbook, setting forth the astrological techniques that made Evangeline Adams one of the most important astrologers of modern times. Her methods can be immensely enlightening to us today. I've also included the horoscopes and stories of many of the people who influenced Adams, so that we may see how not only Evangeline, but also astrology itself grew and developed from the nineteenth to early twentieth centuries in the United States.

Adams was an exceptional astrologer. An Aquarian with the Sun conjunct Mars squaring Pluto, she had a natural affinity for the study, along with great understanding and a probing mind. Her elevated Saturn in the ninth squared Mercury in Pisces, attesting to her constant faith and need to know more. She was broadly read on many topics and deeply knowledgeable about astrology. Her library contained many old and rare volumes, as well as esoteric religious and philosophic works. Three planets and the Ascendant in Pisces, as well as Neptune in the first house, point towards a strong intuition, which supported but did not overshadow her astrological expertise. She began with astrology and practiced palmistry along with it throughout much of her career, but eventually, whether for legal or philosophic reasons, concentrated her efforts primarily on horoscope readings and interpretations.

While Dr. Luke D. Broughton (1828-1898) was responsible for bringing England's astrological tradition to the United States and W.H. Chaney (1821-1903) for training many astrologers across the country, Evangeline Adams (1868-1932) must be seen as the major force behind the popularization of astrology in America. Through her large private practice, mail-order horoscopes, a syndicated radio program, books and publicity efforts, she was able to introduce basic astrology directly to many people who wouldn't otherwise have had access to such specialized information.

Yet concentrating on this broad-based approach left much unsaid. Adams' autobiography, *The Bowl of Heaven* (1926), related her own singular history, and included anecdotes about the famous, tidbits of astrology and her successful astrological predictions. *Astrology, Your Place in the Sun* (1928) presented the essentials: brief descriptions of the signs, planets and houses, along with an elementary method for erecting a horoscope. *Astrology, Your Place Among the Stars* (1930) contained more in-depth information on the planets through Neptune in each sign, with examples from the charts of many celebrities. *Astrology for Everyone* (1931) divided each sign into its decanates, discussed the planets, and offered several essays on various topics of a popular nature. Yet none of these works addressed more sophisticated astrological techniques or theories.

Although Adams had for many years been limiting personal consultations in order to concentrate her energies more fully on her books and writing, her unforeseen death in 1932 (she was said to have predicted it only a few days earlier) left us without much knowledge or understanding of her own techniques. Adams had begun in her last years to lecture both in the United States and abroad, but this was before audio recording was common, and no transcripts seem to have been made. She had no real students outside of her employees, so only the sketchiest of information has been passed down to us through her colleagues and followers.

But we can deduce much about how Adams worked from the information she left us. Her personal consultations were scheduled at half-hour intervals – an amazingly short period of time, which would not allow for diverse techniques or involved calculations. She seemed to like to keep things simple and straightforward. I imagine that Evangeline's Saturn in the ninth house would have forced her to stick to the sound, the tried-and-true, and the obvious.

Adams was found not guilty of fortune-telling in New York City in 1914 because she convinced a judge that she read only the signs of a well-established science; if she could cast a mathematically correct and reproducible chart and base interpretations on the indications provided by published authorities, she was not telling fortunes *per se*. In order to avoid legal trouble in the future, Adams was sure to mention exactly what she was reading when making public pronouncements. We are thus left with capsule descriptions of how she worked, particularly for her forecast of war for the United States from 1942 to 1944 and nationwide financial upheaval from 1927 to 1929.

Adams' advertisement in the *New York City Directory*, citing an 1899 newspaper article, led me to her early forecast for New York City. And church records revealed the time of Evangeline's marriage, thus providing us with the best example we have of how she used electional astrology. The case studies that I've found are consistently illustrative of sound astrological techniques, and we can clearly see Evangeline's transition from nineteenth to twentieth century astrologer. Adams' mundane predictions are indicative of her understanding of larger historic cycles, and thankfully, her craving for publicity has left us with at least some documentation of them.

Nineteenth and early twentieth century astrologers used only nine planets and a few sensitive points to render their judgments. As I personally have a preference for utilizing the basics, I found myself enchanted with the approach of the early moderns. Astrology today is often a stripped-down version of nineteenth century methods. Contemporary astrology accentuates influences rather than events, and often ignores rulerships and essential dignities. Still, most astrologers will recognize, if not be familiar, with nineteenth century techniques. Before psychology had influenced interpretation, astrology provided a solid grounding for those who were stout enough to accept its more serious implications. Today we are apt to smile at the specificity of Adams' 1899 prophecy for New York City or her teacher Catherine Thompson's overly definitive natal delineations. Yet the fact remains that a century ago, astrologers were much more attuned to the practical realities of existence than we are today. They knew the limitations as well as the opportunities promised by the horoscope and were not afraid to exercise judgment in order to help clients better understand their life paths.

What made Evangeline Adams such a great astrologer? In part it was the teachers and friends who influenced her. So I've included their horoscopes to give us a more intimate understanding of the people who shaped this unusual woman. In the Appendix, I've also included some of Adams' previously uncollected works, along with her teachers' writings so that we, too, can experience first-hand what Evangeline herself did as she learned astrology and explored other areas of the occult. These give us a sense of the depth and breadth of Adams' background.

I've tried to uncover timed charts for Adams' teachers, clients and friends, but many years have passed and accurate birth data is always tough to come by. Adams opened her first astrology studio over a hundred years ago; while many public records still exist, birth times were typically not recorded then, and personal records such as family Bibles have been lost. Unfortunately, this leaves us with a number of untimed charts. But accurate birth times or no, I felt it was important to collect the charts of those who touched Adams' life, and we can still learn much from the birthday charts alone. Those who enjoyed my biography, *Foreseeing the Future: Evangeline Adams and Astrology in America* should be pleased to see the horoscopes of their favorite characters in Adams' story.

With the inevitable passage of time, many original sources will continue to disappear. Several of Adams' annual forecasts from the early part of last century were listed in the catalogs of various libraries, but can no longer be found. Contemporary society's fascination with electronic information systems puts the emphasis on new works while neglecting preservation. A project like this will be impossible before many more years go by, as older books and newspaper morgues crumble to dust. Once we lose the ability to consult original sources, we must rely on the opinions of others and cannot form our own judgments.

In spite of its recent popularity, astrology remains on the fringes of Western society, and as such is ruled by Uranus. But if the study is ever again to be regarded as serious and accepted by the community at large, we must also consider Saturn, which demands that we become knowledgeable of our tradition. I'm gratified to have had the opportunity to illuminate a small portion of it here.

A Note on the Charts and Text

I've used Placidus houses in the charts throughout this book, as this system was most commonly used in Evangeline's day. I prefer noon charts to sunrise or solar charts, and have used them whenever I've lacked a time of birth. Charts were generated using Solar Fire 5 software.

Book and magazine excerpts have occasionally been corrected for grammar or spelling, as well as edited for space and clarity, but only when it does not alter the original meaning. Page numbers in Evangeline Adams' autobiography, *The Bowl of Heaven*, refer to the 1970 edition and differ slightly from the earlier edition.

Part I: Who Evangeline Knew

1. An Astrological Education

The famous modern American astrologer Evangeline Adams was born on February 8, 1868 at 8:30 a.m. LMT, in Jersey City, NJ. Adams' father was a railroad man working in Jersey City when she was born, but she grew up in the Boston area and later practiced astrology from New York's Carnegie Hall studios.

Adams is credited with popularizing astrology in America. Her career covered the late nineteenth to early twentieth centuries, and during this period astrology in the U.S. went from a rare commodity to a practice with which most people were at least familiar. Evangeline truly made America astrology conscious.

While her books *Astrology, Your Place in the Sun* (1927) and *Astrology for Everyone* (1931) are introductory texts, her auto-biography, *The Bowl of Heaven* (1926) talks about many astrological topics, and *Astrology Your Place Among the Stars* (1930) discusses the influence of the planets through the signs of the zodiac. These books were reprinted through the 1970's, familiarizing modern students with Evangeline's work. Adams' national radio show, which aired from 1930 to 1931, was one of the most popular shows of its time. Her clients included the naturalist John Burroughs, financier J.P. Morgan, playwright Eugene O'Neill, actress Tallulah Bankhead and mythologist Joseph Campbell.

Adams is well remembered for her eventful life, and her stories have been passed down through generations. She was often said to be descended from presidents John and John Quincey Adams, but she was in fact only related to them, having a common ancestor. Her famous prediction of the Windsor Hotel fire kicked off her career in New York City, as it gave her much publicity. But it seems that Evangeline, herself, was responsible for publicizing her prediction only after the fact. Many magazines have reprinted the fact that Adams "made astrology legal in New York State," but this is not true. Evangeline was tried in a municipal, city, court in 1914 and was acquitted of fortune-telling charges. No laws were changed. Yet the verdict did set a precedent on how the law would be interpreted in New York City in the future.

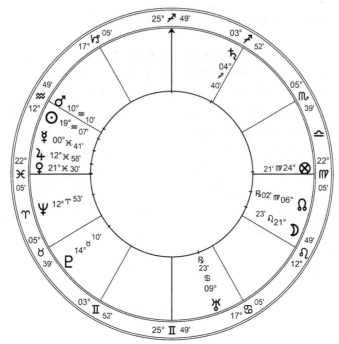

Evangeline Adams
February 8, 1868, 8:30 AM LMT
Jersey City, NJ 40N44 74W04

Source: Adams' birth date is recorded in *A Genealogical History of Henry Adams of Braintree, Massachusetts* (1898), in 1900 Census records, and on her death certificate. Evangeline gives us the time of birth in her autobiography *The Bowl of Heaven*, citing her father's diary.

Adams' Sun and Mars in Aquarius show someone who was naturally receptive to the study of astrology. Throughout her nearly 40-year career, she continued to remain fascinated with the study. With the Sun in the twelfth house, she was primarily a counselor who advised clients through personal consultations. She had strong humanitarian ideals, and always tried to guide others by helping them better understand their birth charts.

A true Aquarian, Adams was also extraordinarily progressive. She was independent and self-supporting at a time when the dream of most women was simply to get married and raise a family. And while necessity forced many women in the 1890's to work, it was extremely rare for anyone, male or female, to make a living through astrology.

Evangeline's Jupiter, although placed in the twelfth house, was a strong planet for her, as it ruled both her Midheaven and Ascendant. In Pisces, one of its ruling signs, it is dignified. The only trine in Adams' chart is from Jupiter to Uranus, the planet of astrology. The placement of Jupiter in the twelfth is often referred to as an "angel on your shoulder" and, indeed, Evangeline eventually overcame all of her difficulties. Her work had wide appeal. In addition to writing and broadcasting, she also lectured and traveled widely, all Jupiter-ruled pursuits.

Perhaps the most important placements in Evangeline's chart were those in the twelfth house and the sign of Pisces, along with Neptune strongly placed. Four planets fell in the twelfth, with Mars on the cusp of this house. The Ascendant, Mercury, Venus and Jupiter were all in Pisces, and gave her a need to help others, as well as a gentleness, impressionability, strong intuition, and the ability to understand symbols. If this wasn't enough, Neptune was right in the first house! Evangeline had originally come to astrology because of a long illness while in her teens. She explored many other meta-physical areas as well; she was actively interested in spiritualism and practiced palmistry for many years.

Evangeline's strong Neptune and her Pisces and twelfth house planets were also responsible for the many myths which have surrounded her. And we don't know much about her personal life. Although she was eager to publicize her own work, she was reserved and unforthcoming when it came to talking about herself. We might even say she was secretive, as Pluto squared her Sun and Mars, and was widely in square to the Moon as well, creating a T-cross.

Pluto fell in her second house and was placed in the sign of Taurus, putting an emphasis on money and finances. Adams' grandfather had been a millionaire, but her father lost most of his money shortly before he died when Evangeline was less than two years old.

Evangeline would follow in her teacher, financial astrologer Catherine Thompson's, footsteps, as her own reputation was partly based on a clientele that included financiers like J.P. Morgan and Charles Schwab. In a 1927 lecture she warned every one to be "extremely cautious in investment and money matters" from 1927 to 1929. When the stock market crashed, she was inundated with much more work.

By the end of her career, Adams was wealthy, charging $50 a half-hour for personal consultations. This may not seem like a large sum now, but consider that many astrologers across the country charge less than $100 an hour *today*. $50 in 1930 could buy a three-piece bedroom set! Evangeline's estate was valued at about $60,000 in 1932, which would be equivalent to nearly $2 million today.

Saturn was also a significant influence in Evangeline's chart, as it was her most elevated planet. Placed in the ninth house in Sagittarius, it highlights her studies and writing, and also her early career as a teacher. Adams' belief in astrology was serious and solid, but, true to Saturn's influence, she had been brought up in the conservative Congregationalist religion. Saturn also points toward Evangeline's forecasting abilities, as it stresses timing and planning for the future. It was also responsible for her legal problems; she was arrested three times and acquitted once, with the other two cases being dismissed.

Placed in the angular fourth house, Uranus, too, was prominent. Adams' unsettled home life included not only the death of her father but growing up with three older brothers! Her mother never re-married, and the family moved several times, living in Jersey City, Andover and Boston, Massachusetts, and Chicago. Evangeline finally settled permanently in New York City in 1905.

Evangeline Adams married a much younger man, George E. Jordan, Jr., when she was 55 years old (Mercury ruled her seventh house and squared Saturn, pointing to her late marriage). Jordan was a promoter who publicized his wife's business. With him, Evangeline wrote her books, began a significant mail-order business, and got her radio show on the air. Her Moon in Leo in the sixth house showed how much she craved attention for her work. She was a workaholic, always eager to talk about astrology, and did much self-promotion and many interviews over the years. In addition, Evangeline's Moon trined her Sagittarius Midheaven, which gave her the need to publicize her ventures to a wide audience. Jupiter placed in Pisces and ruling the Midheaven provided limitless opportunities. Adams' focus throughout her life was education: teaching one and all how astrology could better help them lead purposeful and happier lives.

Evangeline's T-square made up of the Sun, Moon and Pluto created much drama in her life. The Leo Moon rules her fifth house, and she had broken off an engagement with an older, well-to-do man while still young.

Pluto aspects always present complex circumstances, and Adams' eventual marriage involved business interests. We cannot be certain whether Adams married for love, companionship or practical concerns. She continued to vacation alone, with George Jordan at home seeing to their growing business. Jordan was accused of alienating a married woman's affections in a 1931 suit, with much adverse newspaper publicity.

Evangeline had repeatedly forecast a period of war for the United States from 1942 to 1944, but died in 1932 before she could see it come to pass. She reached a national audience and continues to fascinate us over 100 years after she first began practicing astrology. If it were not for her efforts, you might not be reading this book today! Evangeline Adams had a stellar life and career; those who are interested should read my biography, *Foreseeing the Future: Evangeline Adams and Astrology in America* for more.

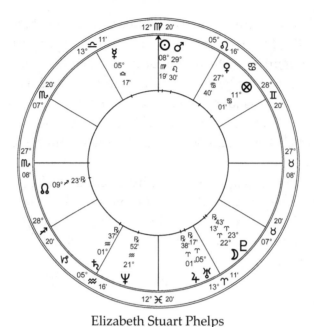

Elizabeth Stuart Phelps
August 31, 1844   Boston, MA 42N22 71W04
Source: Date from *Elizabeth Stuart Phelps* by Carol Farley Kessler;
time is speculative.

Elizabeth Stuart Phelps was Adams' Congregationalist Sunday school teacher in Andover, Massachusetts, and a woman of note in her own right. One of the nineteenth century's most prolific feminist authors, Phelps was an inspiration to Adams, with her natal Jupiter and Uranus falling in Evangeline's first house and closely trining her ninth house Saturn. She brought the exciting and untraditional to the younger woman's life. Phelps was single and self-supporting for many years and Adams followed her lead.

Elizabeth Stuart Phelps was Virgo and an advocate of both homeopathy and animal rights. But the Moon conjunct Pluto in Aries shows a more important concern: the possibility of life after death. Phelps's first novel, *The Gates Ajar*, was published when she was just 24, in 1868, the same year Adams was born. It concerned a woman recovering from the loss of a loved one in the Civil War, and was a best-seller for 30 years.

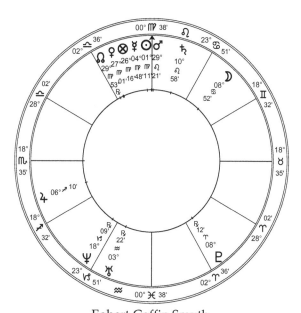

Egbert Coffin Smyth
August 24, 1829 Boston, MA 42N22 71W04
Source: Date from Andover-Newton Theological School records; noon chart.

Egbert Coffin Smyth was one of the theologians that Evangeline knew on Andover Hill, and another insightful interpreter of the narrow Andover creed. Like Phelps, he was a Virgo, and his natal Jupiter conjoined Adams' ninth house Saturn. Adams was struck by his public trial for heresy in 1886-'87. The authorities at Andover Theological Seminary were angry that Smyth and others had published articles contrary to the school's Trinitarian Congregationalist Creed. Evangeline sided with the kindly Professor Smyth against the school; she had just turned 19 and was already thinking very much for herself.

Although the school board convicted Smyth, there were no real consequences, as he remained on staff, being re-appointed as head of the faculty for many years. His appeal of the decision was delayed again and again, and the charges were finally dismissed six years later, after more conservative members of the board had retired or died.

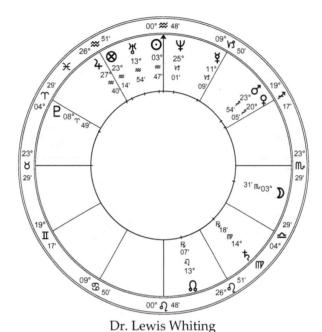

Dr. Lewis Whiting
January 24, 1832 Danvers, MA 42N35 70W56
Source: Date from obituary in the T.L. Bradford scrapbooks; noon chart.

Homeopathy is non-invasive and stimulates the body's natural defense mechanisms, and was a preferred treatment in the nineteenth century. Dr. Lewis Whiting was the homeopath that treated Evangeline while she was dangerously ill for several months in her teens. His Venus and Mars conjoined her Midheaven and trined her sixth house Moon. (We don't know what Adams suffered from. Based on her horoscope and common illnesses of the time, medical astrologer Diane L. Cramer has suggested diphtheria, meningitis or tuberculosis of the spine as possibilities.)

An Aquarian like Evangeline, Whiting was another person who encouraged her to think along the lines of the unusual and different, particularly so as his natal Uranus conjoined her Sun and Mars. Because of Adams' unconventional outlook, Whiting provided her with an introduction to one of his colleagues, Dr. J. Heber Smith.

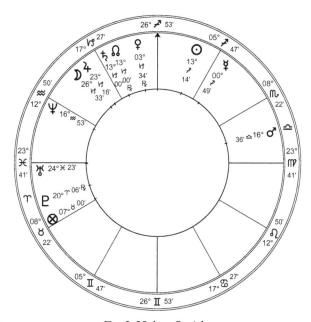

Dr. J. Heber Smith
December 5, 1842   Portland, ME   43N39   70W16
Source: Date from Boston University faculty archives; time is speculative.

Homeopathic physician, college professor and amateur astrologian, J. Heber Smith was a true scholar and well-liked by all who knew him. The *Bostonia* alumni magazine described him as "one of the most popular and versatile members of the faculty with a predilection for occult philosophy." Although "of a quiet but convincing manner," Smith was also said to be a "silver-tongued orator." According to Adams, he had studied Sanskrit and the Eastern religions, and utilized astrology in his medical diagnoses.

J. Heber Smith was Adams' first astrology teacher, as clearly shown by his natal Uranus conjoining her Ascendant. She always held him in high esteem. Adams began studying around 1887, as Saturn in Cancer trined her Venus, and Jupiter in Scorpio trined natal Jupiter and Uranus. Smith died in October of 1898, with transiting Uranus just a few degrees from exactly conjoining Adams' ninth house Saturn.

Dr. Smith's influence is apparent throughout Adams' books, as she often refers to topics in medical astrology. Her apprenticeship was spent erecting and studying the charts of Smith's patients.

The palmist "Cheiro" tells us a little about Dr. Smith in his 1932 *Confessions*:

> This remarkable man worked out a chart of the heavens for every patient; he prescribed for them according to the indications of disease as shown by their planets, and he had more grateful patients than any doctor it has ever been my lot to meet.
>
> He, finally, two years in advance, predicted his own death from the effects of an accident. When the appointed time came, he "put his house in order"; every paper and document was in its place; and so he met his death as calmly for himself as he had often studied it for others. (pp. 179-180)

Smith's obituaries say he died of heart disease on the morning of October 23, 1898, so we may have reason to doubt Cheiro's story. But for many centuries, astrologers have been intrigued with the idea of death and its relation to the birth chart. As a medical man, Dr. Smith would have had more insight into this topic than most. Evangeline, herself, often wrote about her death forecasts, likely another interest sparked by Dr. Smith.

Another homeopath, Dr. George S. Adams (no relation) was the director of the Westborough Insane Hospital, and on the faculty of the Boston University School of Medicine like Dr. Smith. Evangeline studied with him as well, probably along with his student interns, and tells us that,

> Everything in that institution from the care of the most violent patient to the purchase of the best kind of hens to lay the breakfast eggs was done according to the stars. (*Bowl* p. 58)

Psychology was in its infancy in the late nineteenth century, but Evangeline must have gained much insight into human nature and astrology through her work with Dr. Adams. An Aquarian like Evangeline, Adams' Jupiter conjoined her Uranus and trined Jupiter.

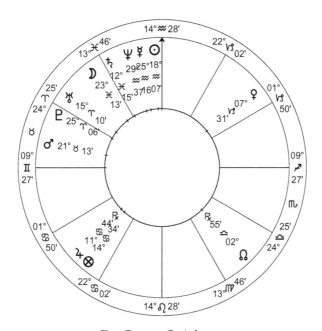

Dr. George S. Adams
February 7, 1848 Norwich, CT 41N31 72W05
Source: Date from the T.L. Bradford Scrapbooks, Hahnemann U.; noon chart.

Evangeline had at one time asked the doctor why people with only one idiosyncrasy were in his institution, while others equally unbalanced were allowed to remain free. His somewhat cynical response quoted in *The Bowl of Heaven* was that,

> Some people are not poor enough to be a burden or rich enough to be gotten out of the way. (p. 61)

Dr. Adams had originally been a machinist, and only later turned to medicine. The Westborough Hospital was one of the first state owned facilities in the country to be run on homeopathic principles, and was said to achieve superior results, according to clippings in The Hahnemann University Archives.

The relationship between Adams and her teacher Catherine Thompson must have been a stormy one, as they both had Mars squaring the other's Mercury. Both Ellen McCaffery in *Astrology, Its History and Influence* and Marie Louise Clemens in her auto-biography assure us that Evangeline took many lessons in astrology from Mrs. Thompson, but these were never publicly acknowledged. For her own part, Thompson wrote to the editors of *Modern Astrology* magazine after Adams' death and erroneously suggested that her pupil was ten years older than she had claimed.

Catherine Thompson was a well-born and bred Englishwoman, who was given the best continental education. Her parents and twin brother all died before she was twenty (her brother died of consumption on August 16, 1874, and had been born half an hour earlier than Catherine). She subsequently married a wealthy American, had two children, and enjoyed large homes in Newport and New York City. After her husband's desertion she "hated men" according to Clemens' account (note her afflicted Mars in the seventh house). Thompson studied astrology with the homeopath Dr. Luke D. Broughton.

With five planets in Taurus, Catherine Thompson was a financial astrologer. It must surely be her influence that steered Evangeline in the same direction, as she would later be known for her many prominent clients in the financial world, such as J.P. Morgan, Charles Schwab and three-term president of the New York Stock Exchange, Seymour Cromwell.

Thompson counseled her cousin, a wealthy coffee broker, who left her in excess of $100,000 in notes. Upon his death in 1922, his estate determined he was of unsound mind when he made the bequest and Thompson lost her subsequent suit. The jury agreed that the astrologer was "a woman of such dominating personality that she had obtained mental control" over her cousin. Although at one time Boston's most well-known and influential astrologer, Catherine Thompson died penniless in 1934.

Thompson's published material on financial astrology is on the simple side when compared with methods developed in the twentieth century (see her "Sugar Map" article on p. 211).

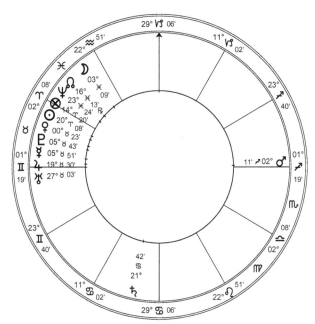

Catherine H. Thompson
April 10, 1858 6:52:01 AM LMT
London, England 51N30 10W00
Source: *The Sphinx* Volume II, No. 1, February 1900, citing the family Bible
(6:50 a.m.) and rectified by W.H. Chaney.

While we will never know for sure exactly what techniques Evangeline, herself, learned, she always claimed that she primarily used the individual birth chart in assessing potential success in investments and speculation.

Louis Hamon called himself a Count, but Evangeline referred to him as "The Great Cheiro." He had read the hands of Sarah Bernhardt, King Edward VII and Oscar Wilde before coming to the United States in 1894. Evangeline studied with him in Boston that winter, as Saturn in Scorpio trined her Mercury, and though she only briefly alludes to it in her autobiography, she practiced palmistry along with astrology for at least the next twenty years.

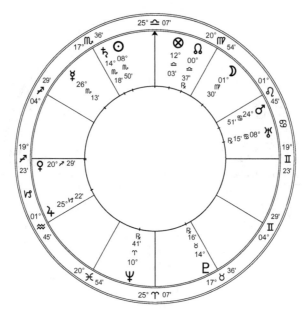

Cheiro (Louis Hamon)
November 1, 1866   10:51 AM LMT
Dublin, Ireland 53N20 6W15
Source: Data from *Astrological Pioneers of America* citing Maurice Wemyss'
Wheel of Life, Vol. 3, p. 31, n. 1.

The relationship was brief, but Cheiro had made a lasting impact: his Saturn formed a grand cross with Adams' Sun, Moon, Pluto T-square.

With a Sagittarius Ascendant and Jupiter in the first house, Cheiro did everything on a grand scale. He traveled widely, charged exorbitant fees, and attracted great attention wherever he went. Evangeline says that women were "crazy about him." (Notice Venus almost exactly conjunct the Ascendant and ruling his fifth house.) When he wasn't claiming to be kidnapped by bandits in Soviet Georgia, beating the bank at Monte Carlo or being attacked by his client's husbands, he wrote books, and many of them. Cheiro married at the age of 54, having finally been irresistibly attracted to a woman with the smallest hands he had ever seen. He eventually became a screenwriter in Hollywood, where he died in 1939.

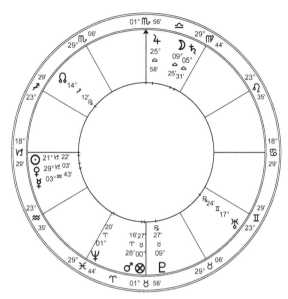

Swami Vivekenanda
January 12, 1863 6:35 AM LMT
Calcutta, India 22N32 88E22
Source: *Astrodatabank* cites the birth record and rates this AA data.

A Hindu monk from India, Swami Vivekenanda attended the Parliament of Religions at the Chicago World's Fair in 1893, stayed in the United States for two years, and returned for another year in 1899, traveling and lecturing on orthodox Vedanta philosophy. As one of the first Hindu representatives to reach our shores, he was a great hit.

The *Encyclopedia of Occultism and Parapsychology* says that Evangeline studied with Vivekenanda, although it gives no other details. She may have attended his lectures in Chicago and Boston, and could even have socialized with him. The Vedanta philosophy, with its emphasis on cycles, transcendentalism, and the possibility of man being at one with the universe, surely appealed to the young astrologer. The Swami's Libra Moon, Jupiter and Saturn fell in Evangeline's seventh house, variously trining her Sun, Mercury and Mars.

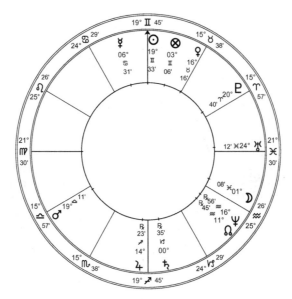

Rev. Dr. Minot J. Savage
June 10, 1841 Norridgewock, ME 44N43 69W47
Source: *New York Times* obituary, May 23, 1918; noon chart.

Evangeline joined a Unitarian church while in Boston and was very much taken with her pastor, the Reverend Dr. Savage. Rev. Savage was known as one of the most direct and forceful pulpit speakers of his day and was also a prolific writer and a member, along with William James, of the Society for Psychical Research. With a wide T-square of Sun, Jupiter and Uranus, he possessed a genuine spirit of inquiry; Mercury out of bounds in declination shows his original views. Evangeline followed his example and attended many séances, claiming to have been involved with,

> ...table-tippers, spirit-photographers, and mediums generally... I have myself had the most extraordinary experiences at séances and spirit demonstrations. (*Bowl*, p. 64)

Savage died at age of 76, a month before an intended marriage. Like Dr. Smith, Savage's Uranus in Pisces conjoined Adams' Ascendant, inspiring her with unusual new ideas.

2. A Life in Astrology

The Magician

Evangeline said that she had been working on a comprehensive astrology book since 1910 or so, but never managed to complete it. She had been looking for someone to co-author or ghost-write the book, and believed she had found him in the notorious British magician and occultist Aleister Crowley. Crowley had come to the U.S. late in 1914 and met Adams at the home of a mutual friend. This began what he called "a lengthy association."

Though the partnership did not last, both gained in the relationship: Adams had begun her book in earnest, and Crowley further developed his astrology. Their association continued into 1916, and coincided with the transit of Uranus in conjunction with Adams' natal Sun, described in the *Evangeline Adams Guide for 1933* as,

> ...a propitious time for dealings with people of unusual and original ability... This aspect frequently causes one to be started upon the road which may lead to their greatest accomplishment. (*1933* p. 261-262)

Uranus at the time also conjoined Crowley's Saturn and opposed Uranus from the cusp of his eighth house. He felt that Adams had taken advantage of him, and would go on to publish "How Horoscopes are Faked" in 1917 in *The International,* a German *avant-garde* arts magazine in the U.S., which has been reproduced in *The General Principles of Astrology* (2002). In this scathing critique Crowley portrays Adams as a money-grubber who took advantage of her clients:

> The laws of the State of New York are supposed to prohibit fortune-telling, and they are, indeed, applied with great severity so far as the little fish are concerned. But the big fish, the most conscienceless swindlers of all, seem to dodge the police. A lot of bluff has been put up about "scientific" astrology. I propose to show how the game is really worked.

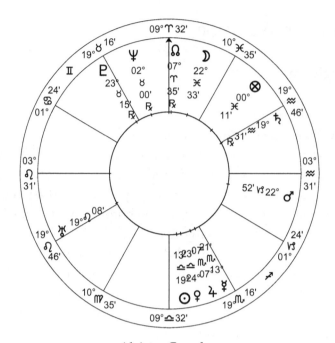

Aleister Crowley
October 12, 1875 11:16:39 PM GMT
Leamington Spa, England 52N18 1W31
Source: Hymenaeus Beta in *The General Principles of Astrology*
cites Fernando Pessoa's rectified time.

Crowley came from a wealthy background and had already been involved with and headed several magical societies, written poetry, prose and erotica, and published his own occult magazine, *The Equinox*. A difficult personality (his chart holds a wide grand cross made up of Mercury, Saturn, Uranus and Pluto), his Leo Ascendant loved the publicity garnered by flouting conventional authority and flaunting his sexuality. Yet his constant adage, "do what thou wilt," had more to do with being true to one's own self than anything else.

With Mercury conjunct Jupiter in Scorpio, Crowley was a brilliant and perceptive man. Although he had not concentrated his energies exclusively on astrology before his work with Adams, he quickly studied the subject in depth.

In retrospect, we might wonder why Evangeline would associate herself with such a man of extremes. Yet her Sun fell right in his seventh house. His Sun and Venus were in her seventh and his Moon conjoined her Ascendant: they were ideal partners in many ways. Adams' lucky Jupiter trine Uranus became a grand trine with the addition of Crowley's Mercury and Jupiter, so their intellectual association must have been stimulating. Yet Adams' Sun, Moon, Pluto T-square fell right onto Crowley's critical grand cross: while they shared many things in common, ultimately the relationship became too difficult and broke down.

Hymenaeus Beta has reconstructed Crowley and Adams' work in *The General Principles of Astrology*. It includes the bulk of what was originally published as Adams' *Astrology, Your Place Among the Stars* and *Astrology, Your Place in the Sun*, as well as Crowley's text on Uranus and Neptune through the houses and Neptune's aspects with the other planets, which Adams never published. This is excellent work, and anyone interested in Adams or Crowley should read it.

Over twelve years passed from her association with Crowley before Evangeline herself had the original texts edited, re-written and published; while the two clearly worked together, it is sometimes easy to see where credit is due each author. The overall astrological concepts were probably based on Adams' many years of experience; the writing itself was Crowley's. Crowley was also highly educated, with an excellent grasp of the classics and the history of astrology and the occult. The descriptions of the charts from *A Thousand and One Notable Nativities* that make up most of the examples in *Stars* show a European bias, as Hymenaeus Beta points out. Where Crowley at times brings in a host of occult symbolism from various sources, Adams stays closer to home, and she is always to the point. He is not afraid to risk all while she is typically more cautious.

Their extraordinarily different tones are at times also apparent. Adams, with all of her Aquarius and Pisces, is always objective and detached from the work. Crowley, thinking through his Scorpio

Mercury and Jupiter, can be too passionate at times. After examining the relative merits of historic giants whose charts held aspects between Mercury and Neptune, he cannot resist continuing with a brutally honest critique:

> Most of the examples that we have given impress us rather as brilliant than as profound. Gladstone was too clever to be a real statesman; Edison never made a discovery in abstract science; Petrarch is not in the first flight of poets; the star of Coleridge has but three narrow rays; Luther was not a deep theologian; Ruskin was but an artist manque; Napoleon never cut at the roots of his political oaks; Dumas is but a narrator; Savonarola never did more than scourge the symptoms of the evil he attacked; Byron never wrote first-rate poetry; Marston is but a sorry rhymester; Wilde and Shaw have done nothing immortal; Harmsworth [a British newspaper proprietor] is a byword for shallowness, stupidity and sensationalism; du Maurier was a hack, Steiner a quack. Balzac, it is true, was the greatest novelist that trine has yet brought forth; but the... gods must be made to speak in order to explain his capacity and energy and his ever-crescent and immortal fame.

In a like manner, Crowley's strong personal bias can sometimes get in the way of accurate judgments:

> Tennyson had also Mars conjoined with Uranus, making him a toady and selfish scoundrel.

> The feeble, dreamy, almost imbecile W.B. Yeats has Mars and Neptune trine; but the combination gives him power in a shadow-world of his own.

With her medical astrology background, Adams can undoubtedly be credited with the specific references to illness throughout the text. But in the final analysis, my own feeling is that this was a true collaboration – and we may never know exactly how much each contributed.

The subsequent excerpts only appear in Crowley's *The General Principles of Astrology* and not in Evangeline's books. These statements are quite authoritative – but whose authority is it?

Conjunctions, even of the most favorable planets, are not to be trusted unless they have support from other parts of heaven.

Opposition generally means conflict and exhaustion; both planets lose in force. The quartile aspect means attack; both planets become more brutal. (This is not always necessarily bad: for example, Sun quartile Mars in a question of health might seem a rude robustness.) The sextile aspect is friendly, bringing out the softer qualities of both planets.

The trine aspect resembles the alliance of two great kings. They mutually support and defend one another; the strength of both is brought out in its best form. This aspect is more important when the planets are large and slow-moving.

It is almost safe to say that no horoscope is really first rate without good aspects or strong positions of the male planets Sol, Mars or Saturn. Jupiter is too comfortable to move the world alone; he likes things as they are.

When there is any dispute, so to say, among the other planets, the tenth house assumes primary importance.

Essential dignity [of a planet] should first be regarded by reference to the sign in which he is situated and to his aspects, before his influence in the house is investigated; for his nature must be modified by these circumstances.

The "Major Key to Astrology" (below) is from Adams' most important work, *Astrology, Your Place Among the Stars*, and is nearly identical to parts of a similarly titled piece by Crowley.

A glance at the horoscopes of the greatest men of whom we have record shows that, generally speaking, the planets form exact or very close aspects, and also – this is the important point – that all, or very nearly all, the planets are interwoven. Sometimes we find two or three complexes in a nativity, perhaps even four; and these have no close relation with one another. Such horoscopes are those of commonplace people. It is as if they had several strands in their nature, which had not been properly interwoven. As a result, there are times when one is at work in its own feeble way; then it is forgotten, and another comes into operation. The lack of continuity is fatal to the performance of any constructive work. If such a person should acquire fame, it is the result of some action suddenly conceived and executed, or because of an apparent accident.

Two men might have identical aspects and yet be utterly different just because in one case the Lord of the Ascendant was Mars and in the other Venus. It is not always easy to divine the secret pivot on which a complex swings. The Lord of the Ascendant is usually the cardinal point, but if there be several planets or even one very strong planet rising, he may be overwhelmed by them or it and his place in heaven, as it were, usurped. And it is of the utmost importance that this fundamental planet be detected with accuracy; for it makes all the difference in the world whether we regard the other planets as modifying Saturn or Jupiter. If the native be a Saturnian at heart, the trine of Jupiter will favor his selfish plans; if a Jupiterian, the trine of Saturn will restrict and balance his enthusiasms. The conjunction of the Sun and Venus which made Shelley so glorious an incarnation of Light and Beauty would hardly have acted in that way had Scorpio, not Sagittarius, been his Ascendant. (*Stars* pp. vii-x)

The following aphorisms are taken primarily from *Astrology, Your Place Among the Stars*. They are surprisingly simple, but are given the typical Adams (or Crowley!) ring of authority.

It cannot be too strongly emphasized again that an analysis of the meaning of every factor in Astrology is dependent upon its relation to every other factor. It is from the sum of the forces and not from each one of them separately judged, that an analysis is made.

The four bodies whose influence and position have most to do with human character are the two luminaries, that is the Sun and the Moon, and the two minor planets, Mercury and Venus, whose orbits lie within that of the earth.

Where the Sun is strong, it does not, of itself, imply more than the vigor of powerful animal life, which enables the native to reap the rewards of favorable planetary aspects and, conversely, to suffer and endure the buffets of adverse influences. When the Sun is weak, no amount of benefits from the other planets will counteract the affliction. (from *Astrology for Everyone*)

The Moon's position is the focal point wherein sense, mind, and emotion meet in the formation of character.

Indeed, we may say that the average person is largely judged in life by the sign position of his Moon, and that this position may even act as a completely qualifying influence, if evil aspects interfere, and thus bring out some of the lower phases of the sign influence. We have thousands of instances, in astrological record, of such complete modification of the personality through the Moon position that the whole life was totally wrecked; and it is not difficult to see why this should be so, for, if the Moon primarily governs the Sensorium, that is, the sight, hearing, smell, taste, and touch, it necessarily is sufficiently strong absolutely to dominate the man. If we remember that all knowledge, all information, all preference, all judgment, come into the man first of all through the use of his senses, that the sight, hearing, smell, taste and touch are the mental mouth, without which the rational stomach can receive no food, we can understand why the Moon can completely block a life's development.

It will be seen that the Moon is more sensitive to its sign than the Sun or any of the planets.

It is probably fair to say that any serious affliction of the Moon dulls the acuteness of at least one of the senses. As a general rule, a single minor affliction produces only minor consequences.

The proper and best influence upon Mercury is Saturn, and without his steadying hand to hold him in tutorship to a profounder wisdom, Mercury may be frivolous and vain. We must urge upon the student to regard carefully the aspects to this planet, but not to accept them as operative unless very close. At the same time whatever aspects may exist will not alter the essential character of Mercury, as determined by the sign in which he is placed.

It is essentially, and first of all, the private life that Venus influences.

Mars represents the muscular system; it is often found that a weak brain goes with great development of physical strength, and *vice versa*. It might even occur that the whole of the higher faculties might be harmonious and strong, yet fail to make good, owing to the lack of practical energy, boldness, and capacity for rather brutal work. The material plane continually presents obstacles to the higher nature; Mars is the force which pushes such obstacles aside, or demolishes them.

Even though there may be adverse aspects operating in one's chart during a friendly aspect of Jupiter to the Sun, this will have a very modifying influence and bring directly or indirectly good conditions out of what may appear to be adversity.

In the days when a man was either a lord or a serf, a knight or an innkeeper, it was comparatively easy to determine with exactness a man's vocation. In modern days, however, there are thousands of different and characteristic types of employment. While Jupiter is the key to the type of work which may bring a man money or profit, it does not necessarily follow that it is the kind of vocation for which he has the greatest inclination.

Unless Saturn be dignified nobly – the best of all his dignities is illumination by the Sun – he represents malefic force.

Whenever under the influence of Saturn, it is well to take things very much as they come, live one day at a time and go along the line of intelligent non-resistance. By refusing to force issues one will come out much better in the long run. On the other hand, if one insists on putting through things at any cost, one is likely to make bad matters worse and be in danger of making very unwise moves, pushing aside opportunities and failing to embrace things which are worthwhile.

In the few years during which Uranus has been under observation, it has been found that, if afflicted, it is the source of incurable organic diseases, collapse of fortune, and individual as well as national destruction. It is demonstrable that, in inharmonious nativities, evil Uranian influences, both through transits and directions, have brought about headlong destruction from bad habits, misdirected affection, illicit connections before or after legal marriage; according to the signification of the place of radical affliction in the horoscope.

Neptune causes diseases which come as the result of worry, and all illnesses of an insidious and wasting character. A general weakness and irritability of disposition may manifest itself in hysteria. Painful and intractable, though not dangerous, disorders may be the source of much discomfort. Those born strongly under Neptune should abstain from reading books on *materia medica*, as they are so susceptible to suggestion as to imagine that they evidence symptoms of every disease they read about. They should avoid dwelling on their ills, real or imaginary, and not form the habit of dosing themselves or taking patent medicines.

The weak part of the body is indicated by the sign involved, and the type of disease threatened by the planet which menaces the mischief. The native can therefore take measures to obviate the peculiar risk to which his attention is thus drawn.

A Marriage Made in Heaven?

Mercury rules Adams' seventh house; when Uranus conjoined it during 1920, she had the first contact with her future husband (she was 52 years old at the time). They married in April of 1923, two months after Uranus' last conjunction with her ruler, Jupiter. Adams had said of this aspect in her *Guide for 1933* that,

> This is an extremely powerful aspect, which only occurs once in a lifetime, and which can work out advantageously, or just the reverse. If you confine your efforts to your legitimate business, then you will do the right thing, for you are more likely to be in harmony with yourself and the constructive forces of the Universe than you have been in many years.
>
> The action of Uranus is sudden and violent and often causes one to attract schemers and to suffer from very undesirable people. If any ventures are laid before you, particularly involving your money or reputation, then look into them very skeptically. If you discover the slightest indication of intrigue or questionable ethics, or if the people involved show any tendency to work just within the law, then you may be sure they are either trying to trade on your reputation for honesty in order to get their schemes accepted, or to get your money...
>
> This is likely to be a very hectic period for you financially. Make no changes without first investigating thoroughly. This is a period in your life when an ounce of caution is worth a pound of cure. It may be a very critical time, but the actual outcome will depend entirely upon the decisions you now make. Be sure they are wise ones. (*1933* p. 297-298)

It seems as if Adams waited until this aspect was actually past to tie the knot, but she should have listened to her own advice. My feeling is that Evangeline truly loved her husband, though most everyone else disliked him. The staff resented him and he created fresh difficulties in Evangeline's often tenuous relationship with her family. A much-publicized scandal in 1931 linked him romantically with one of their employees.

As Uranus went on to conjoin Adams' Venus and Ascendant during 1924 and 1925, there were other major life changes. Her husband joined as her business partner and they began work on her autobiography. Shortly after the final conjunction in January of 1926, plans were laid for a huge astrological enterprise, and their office space was tripled.

Evangeline always romanticized her meeting with George E. Jordan, Jr. Early in 1920, as the story goes, a client had consulted her regarding a business deal, also providing the horoscope of his prospective partner. She was reportedly so much interested in the other man's chart that she asked to be introduced to him, even though he was over twenty years her junior! Adams subsequently told the *New York Mirror* that,

> All my life I've known that a man born with that particular pattern of the stars at birth would come into my life some day.

It's difficult to imagine what "pattern" she may be talking about, though we lack a time of birth for Jordan. While the couple shared a Leo Moon, the actual comparison is challenging. Jordan's Mercury, Mars, Saturn, Neptune, Pluto T-square aggravated Eva's Mercury square Saturn. And her Moon neared a conjunction with his Saturn. The tall, gaunt and painfully thin Jordan made an odd match for the very short, plump Adams.

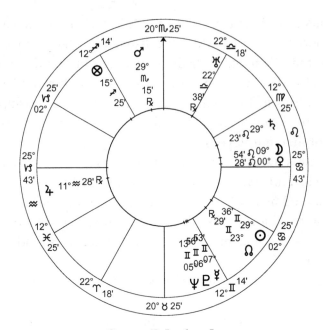

George E. Jordan, Jr.
June 20, 1890 Foxboro, MA 42N04 71W07
Source: Birth certificate; time is speculative.

But without Jordan, Adams would probably not be remembered today. He acted as her business manager after their marriage in 1923, spearheading the production of her books and greatly expanding her business through mail order horoscopes, much publicity, and Adams' popular radio show.

Jordan inherited a fortune after his wife's death in 1932, but by that time was rumored to be a confirmed alcoholic and unable to continue the business without his wife's expertise and charisma.

Friends and Associates

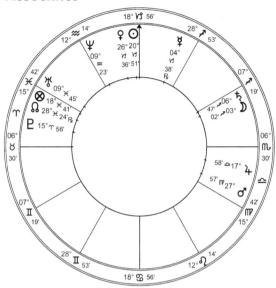

Franklin Simmons
January 11, 1839 Lewiston, ME 44N06 70W13
Source: *Who Was Who in American Art*; noon chart.

Franklin Simmons was the wealthy gentleman that Dr. Smith had foreseen, who proposed to Evangeline, probably around 1888 or 1889. Adams tells us in *The Bowl of Heaven* that he was, "both socially and astrologically congenial." Though 30 years older, Simmons' Sun and Venus sextiled Evangeline's Venus. Their Mercurys were also sextile, and his Uranus conjoined her Jupiter. This must have been a pleasant and intriguing relationship. Simmons was a famous American sculptor who had relocated to Rome, and he wanted to take Evangeline away to a life of leisure in his *palazzo*. Since Adams loved her work, this was not appealing. And despite their compatibility, Evangeline felt that Simmons' own chart presented a problem:

I saw, the first time I looked at Sir Franklin's chart, that his Moon, governing his relations with women, was badly afflicted, a condition which suggested that our relationship would probably end either in my death or my unfaithfulness… I found either alternative most undesirable. (*Bowl* p. 154)

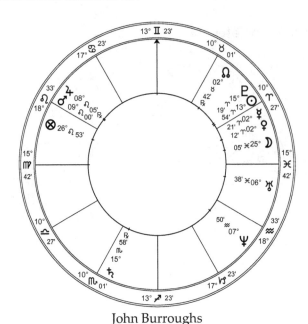

John Burroughs
April 3, 1837 Roxbury, NY 40N34 73W53
Source: In *The Bowl of Heaven*, p. 81-82, Evangeline describes Burroughs' chart. The
date is from the *Dictionary of American Biography*.

Famous naturalist and author John Burroughs first came to see
Adams as a client:

> That meeting in Boston was the beginning of a close friendship
> which resulted in many happy, helpful hours of study and investigation,
> sometimes here in my studio, sometimes at Mr. Burroughs' beloved
> Slabsides, during which my fine old friend and I, he from the naturalist's
> viewpoint, and I from the astrologer's, sought the truth about life. (*Bowl*
> p. 40)

Burroughs' Moon conjoined Evangeline's Ascendant and his Sun
fell right on her first house Neptune, so he supported her. Adams
quoted the naturalist as saying,

> Why do I believe in astrology?... Why shouldn't I? Everything in the
> universe influences everything else, so, naturally, the stars must
> influence man. (*Bowl* p. 41)

In the following excerpt from his book, *Signs and Seasons*, the man with the Pisces Moon relates the sky to the sea:

There seems to be something more cosmic, or shall I say astronomic, in the sea than on the shore. Here you behold the round back of the globe: the lines are planetary. You feel that here is the true surface of the sphere, the curving, delicate sides of this huge bubble... You are upon the smooth disk of the planet, like a man bestriding the moon. Under your feet runs the line of the earth's rotundity, and round about you the same curve bounds your vision.

This is a part of the vague fascination of the shore; 'tis the boundary of two worlds. With your feet upon the present, you confront aboriginal time and space. If we could reach the point in the horizon where the earth and sky meet, we might find the same fascination there. In the absence of this the best substitute is the beach.

We seem to breathe a larger air on the coast. It is the place for large types, large thoughts. 'Tis not farms, or a township, we see now, but God's own domain. Possession, ownership, civilization, boundary lines cease, and there within reach is a clear page of terrestrial space, as unmarred and as unmarrable as if plucked from the sidereal heavens. (pp. 162-164)

Another Boston friend was the poet Ella Wheeler Wilcox. In her sales brochure, Adams quoted Wilcox as saying, "If you want to be astonished – let Evangeline S. Adams cast your horoscope."

Wilcox wrote a poem a day for nationwide syndication, many of them sentimental, as her Cancer Sun enjoyed. Her Mercury and Venus in Gemini squaring Neptune also seem apt symbols.

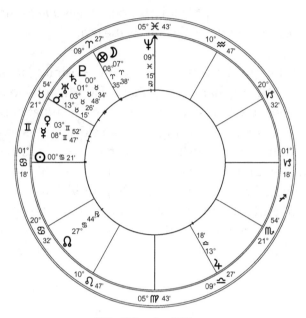

Ella Wheeler Wilcox
June 22, 1851 4:30 AM LMT
Johnson Junction, WI 43N03 88W47
Source: Lois Rodden in *Profiles of Women* cites Church of Light files for this data.

Wilcox's poem, "The Winds of Fate" had a philosophic message; Adams included it above her signature at the end of all of her mail order work and in *The Bowl of Heaven*:

One ship drives east and another drives west
With the self-same winds that blow.
   'Tis the set of the sails
   And not the gales
   Which tell us the way to go.

Like the winds of the sea are the ways of fate
As we voyage along through life.
   'Tis the set of the soul
   That decides its goal
   And not the calm or the strife.

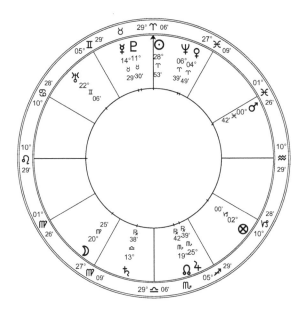

Richard Harding Davis
April 18, 1864 New York, NY 40N43 74W00
Source: *Dictionary of American Biography*; noon chart.

Adams occasionally had clients who simply seemed to want to annoy her:

> A man came to see me some years ago whose sole purpose, so far as I could make out, was to make me "mad." And he succeeded. Everything I said he contradicted – until finally I dropped his chart and launched into a passionate defense of my beloved science. This was evidently just what he wanted. He sat back listening intently. (*Bowl* p. 195)

For his own part, Richard Harding Davis described Evangeline thus,

> They saw her drawn to her full height; the color flown from her face, her deep, brooding eyes flashing. She was like one, by some religious fervor, lifted out of herself, exalted. When she spoke her voice was low, tense. It vibrated with tremendous, wondering indignation. (*Vera, the Medium* p. 150-151)

Davis was a famous novelist and war correspondent who visited Adams around 1907, supposedly to gather information for his book, *Vera, the Medium*. He didn't have much difficulty in aggravating Evangeline with his objections to astrology. His Mars in Pisces exactly conjoining her Mercury shows his aggressiveness toward her thinking. Her Mars also squared his Mercury, so the words were heated on both sides. (We saw something similar in Adams' relationship with her teacher, Catherine Thompson.)

The material included in this chapter on the transits of the planets is the work of Dr. Heber Smith of Boston, who was the teacher of Miss Evangeline Adams. It is reported that Mrs. Julie Pontin, the rival of Miss Adams, paid $150 for a typewritten copy of this material.

So said Sydney Omarr in his book, *My World of Astrology* (p. 309). "The Transits of the Planets" was not written by Dr. Smith, but does appear to represent his work. (See p. 203 in Appendix IV for a sample.)

Unfortunately for Pontin, little is remembered about her, so she seems to have been very much eclipsed by Adams. Her fixed angular grand cross involving Mercury, Mars, Saturn, Uranus and Neptune probably made for a difficult early life, disappointments in marriage and some ups and downs in her career. And with Mars in Scorpio in her first house ruling the seventh, she could easily have become envious of the accomplishments of her more successful contemporary.

Yet there are many lovely things in this horoscope. A kite is found within the grand cross, and trines from Jupiter in the eleventh and the Sun in the ninth house in mixed mutual reception promise much satisfaction from friends and study. Pontin lectured on metaphysical topics and was an editor for an occult publication.

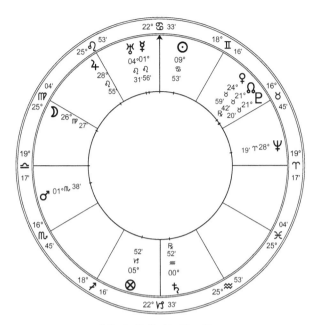

Marie Juliette Pontin
July 1, 1873 12:58 PM LMT
New York, NY 40N43 74W00
Source: Holden & Hughes cite Howard Hammitt's
Chronological Nativities, Vol. 2 p. 41.

But $150 in 1912 or '13, when the "Transits" piece was written, was an enormous sum! (In 1913, Henry Ford had just raised his assembly line workers' salaries to $5 a week, a revolutionary high wage. It would take over seven months of this full salary to pay the $150 for the "Transits" work.)

Pontin could afford it. With Venus conjunct Pluto in Taurus in the eighth house, she had probably come into quite a lot of money and invested wisely, occasionally spending lavishly on knowledge, since her Venus squared Jupiter.

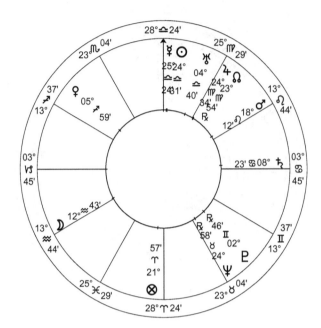

Vahdah Olcott Bickford
October 17, 1885 Norwalk, OH 41N15 82W37
Source: Edward L. Dearborn collection; noon chart.

Vahdah Olcott Bickford (born Ethel Lucretia Olcott) said she'd been Evangeline Adams' only assistant from 1915 to 1924. This was the time before Adams' great business expansion, so the claim may be true. Her Libra Sun trined Adams' Sun and her Moon conjoined her employer's Sun, making for a solid connection.

But Evangeline left legacies to three of her other valued assistants. Why not Vahdah? Bickford's Saturn square Uranus aggravated Adams' natal Uranus-Neptune square. And her Pluto turned Adams' Mercury square Saturn into a T-square as well. Vahdah's Neptune fell in Evangeline's second house, and squared her employer's Sun and Moon. The two women also had their Moons conjoining each other's Mars, aggravating their emotions. Despite the basic Sun-Moon compatibility, this appears to have been a complex relationship, with no other details known.

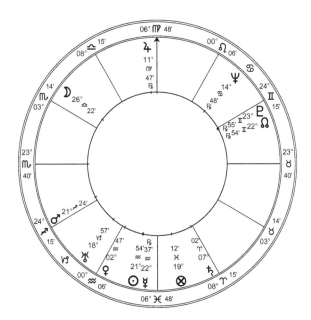

Joseph L. Mankiewicz
February 11, 1909 1:15 AM
Wilkes-Barre, PA 41N15 75W53
Source: *Astrodatabank* rates this "A" data, quoting Mankiewicz himself.

The Academy Award winning writer and director of *All About Eve*, *A Letter to Three Wives* and *The Barefoot Contessa* entered Columbia University at age fifteen and worked for Evangeline Adams before he graduated in 1928. Evangeline kept writers on staff for her monthly planetary forecasts and other written work. But they probably contributed to her books as well. Since she had been unable to launch her book projects on her own and had made an abortive start with Aleister Crowley, perhaps Mankiewicz was one of those who stepped in. *The Bowl of Heaven* was written around 1924, about the time he started working there.

Another Aquarian like herself, Joseph's Venus was near Adams' Mars, and his Moon fell in her seventh house of partner-ships. His Saturn in her first house trined her Saturn in Sagittarius in the ninth, so his efforts could well have solidified her plans for publication.

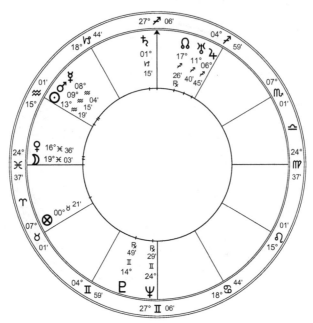

Carroll Righter
February 2, 1900 9:00 AM EST
Salem, NJ 39N34 75W28
Source: *Astrodatabank* cites Righter and rates this "A" data.

Carroll Righter's parents were friends of Adams' and had her read the boy's chart when he was just fourteen. She felt he'd be exceptionally gifted as an astrologer. No wonder! His Aquarius and Pisces placements mirrored her own. "I didn't believe her," Righter later recalled. "In fact, I thought the whole thing was idiotic." (*Current Biography Yearbook* 1972 p. 370-372). He went on to get a law degree, disliked the field, and also suffered from various sports injuries.

By the time Righter was around thirty, however, he'd con-vinced himself there was something to astrology:

> I thought I could convince myself there was nothing in it, but after sixteen years of study I wound up believing in it.

In 1937, Righter's back ailment required a cast, and his health created such problems that his doctor felt he wouldn't live for more than six months. Carroll noted his fortunate Jupiter in Sagittarius in the ninth house and felt it suggested "physical protection in the Southwest." Moving to southern California for therapy, he im-proved within the year. Righter turned professional in 1939 after meeting Marlene Dietrich at a Hollywood party, and the movie business provided many subsequent clients.

Jupiter in Sagittarius in the ninth house, of course, promises success through publishing as well. Carroll Righter wrote seven books, and by 1960 his daily horoscope column reached thirty million households across the U.S. He died in 1988.

Sidney K. Bennett was another Aquarian with Venus and Jupiter in Pisces in the twelfth house like Evangeline. About 25 years her junior, Bennett, or "Wynn" as he called himself, also practiced astrology, and taking Adams' lead, worked out of a suite at the Carnegie Hall Studios beginning in 1931.

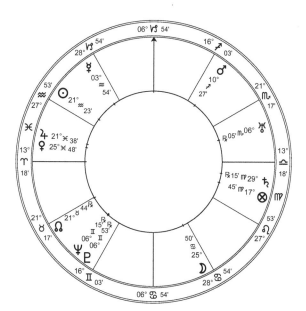

Sidney K. Bennett
February 10, 1892 9:00 AM CST
Chicago, IL 41N51 87W39
Source: Lois Rodden's *Astrodata III* cites Bennett himself.

When Evangeline's book, *Astrology for Everyone*, came out in 1931, Wynn denounced it at an Astrologers Guild meeting, claiming Adams was misinforming the public with Sun sign astrology. He was reminded by the group of his own column in the *New York Daily News* and soon settled down (as described in C.P. Tobey's book, p. 359).

Wynn's Ascendant was ruled by Mars, Evangeline's by Jupiter. He never received quite the acclaim the older astrologer had. He became well known for a prediction of financial turmoil in March of 1933, when President Roosevelt declared a bank holiday. He's best remembered for his Key Cycle for solar returns and *Wynn's Astrology Magazine*, which he published for a decade or more.

When Evangeline first appeared on the radio in 1930, she was sponsored by Forhan's toothpaste. They came up with a merchandising gimmick and offered free mini horoscope readings for box top coupons. After three months on the air, Adams reported that she'd received 150,000 requests. Many who received the sample reading no doubt returned as paying customers for a more in-depth written portrait or perhaps even a personal consultation.

Lewis Mumford and his wife sent away for free readings in July of 1930. Mumford was a well-known author and teacher who wrote about art, city planning and social history. This one-page summary obviously goes one step beyond simple Sun signs:

You were born under the astrological sign Libra, symbolized by the Balance. Venus, the Goddess of Love and Beauty, is the dominant planet of that sign. Libra people have a fine sense of harmony and proportion. They are natural arbitrators. They make excellent judges, bankers, diplomats, architects and engineers. They often succeed in artistic careers. In more commercial pursuits, however, they are sometimes handicapped by lack of decision, due to their tendency to balance one sign against the other.

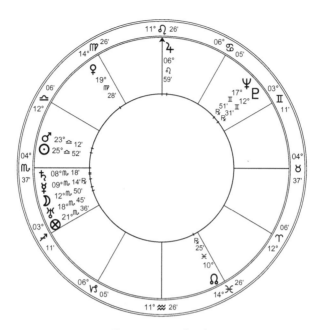

Lewis Mumford
October 19, 1895 7:00 AM EST
Flushing, NY 40N45 73W49
Source: *Astrodatabank* sources Mumford's "Sketches from Life" Beacon, NY, 1982 and
rates this "B" data.

Libra people are also the best of company. This statement applies
with special force to those born in your part of the sign, because
Jupiter, which was influential in the astrological heavens at the time
of your birth, makes for popularity. You are agreeable to all, but
especially affable to friends and associates of congenial tastes. You are
generous and kind, beloved for your amiability and respected for
your justice and probity. You are a faithful friend and a generous
enemy. With such favoring planets as Venus and Jupiter influential in
your horoscope there is no good reason why you should not achieve
success both in love and money. Venus rules the love life. Jupiter
confers honor and fame. Both are favorable to success and wealth. To
take advantage of these rich opportunities, Libra has given you a
sensitive, well-balanced mind and an appreciation of the finer things
of life.

The tendency of people born in your sign to weigh both sides of a question too carefully and too long should be offset in your case by the invigorating influence of Jupiter. At the same time, it is the one characteristic about which you should be continually on guard. Force yourself to decision and action. The sensitive nature of your sign also has its dangers. It is favorable to your highest ethical and aesthetic development because it makes you abhor the vulgar and the crude. But it also leads to unnecessary suffering and mental anguish. Libra's scales go up and down. Unless the greatest care is exercised, they tip too easily and too far. You are "way up" or "way down." You must guard against this tendency so that your naturally good judgment may not be obscured by temporary elation and depression and your social gifts hampered by moods.

You may not be robust in appearance. Libra people incline to beauty rather than brawn. But you should possess an extremely sound constitution. Look out for trouble in the kidneys and the lumbar region; these are your weak spots, if you have any. Avoid violent exercise. Don't strain the back. Above all, don't wobble. Decide and act!

Mumford's daughter said, "This seems rather apt: but compare it with the nonsense in mother's horoscope!" Unfortunately, we don't have Mrs. Mumford's birth data and we all know that Sun sign astrology can at times be misleading. But Evangeline was always partial to Aquarians like herself and Mrs. Mumford. Was she describing herself? Perhaps she exaggerates a bit for sentimental reasons, or maybe she felt that Aquarians had gotten a bad rap because of the Sun's detriment in this sign. If this were the case, she, herself, is being more Piscean than Aquarian!

You were born in one of the best signs of the zodiac – and in one of the best parts of that sign. You are what astrology calls an Aquarian child, but you are more blessed than most Aquarians because Mercury, the planet which rules the intellect, was dominant in the heavens when you were born.

You will seek and enjoy learned society. And you will turn naturally to scientific and philosophical pursuits in which depth of intellect is essential to success. All Aquarians are naturally of a humanitarian nature. Their great pleasure is to do good to others. They see the world whole. And they rise above personal desires and selfish aims. You are like that. But because of the special influence of Mercury, you, more than most people, have the power to carry these traits toward a successful conclusion.

You will excel not only as a physician, teacher, writer, social worker, nurse or inventor, but you may even become interested in astronomy, astrology, and occult research. You possess an intuition which is akin to prophecy. In fact, it is often taken for prophecy. Your health is generally good. If properly guarded, there is small chance of serious impairment; but your mind will be so active that you may neglect to keep your body active, too. Take plenty of exercise. Keep the organs functioning freely. Look to the care of your feet and legs. Regulate your diet so as to avoid rheumatic difficulties. You will always enjoy a good reputation – and deservedly. You are essentially loyal. Your devotion, once given, knows no limit in service. Your chief danger is that you may overtax yourself in your effort to give too much. Don't forget that you must save your strength for the world's work. You do not need to be warned against sloth or changefulness. You work hard and to the end. Your success is won that way. It is not the overnight kind. It comes slowly, but it lasts. Eighty percent of the people in the Hall of Fame were born under your sign. You value money not for itself but for the good it will do. Your greatest reward – and one you will surely get if you are true to your sign – is the knowledge that you have helped others to get more out of life.

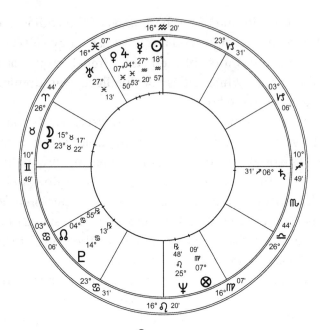

Sunaqua
February 8, 1927 New York, NY 40N43 74W00
Source: E. Adams letter of May 1, 1928; noon chart.

"Do I ever make mistakes?" exclaimed Evangeline Adams, laying down her astrological charts and shaking her bobbed gray hair with an emphasis which caused a young Belgian griffon to roll off a couch, an accident which changed the subject temporarily. The astrologer had just bought this puppy, because she could not resist its horoscope. It is a dog of destiny. It can hardly help being another Rin-Tin-Tin or Bob, Son of Battle. Miss Adams was shopping for a Pekinese, but on learning the hour of the griffon's nativity and finding the heavens sensationally auspicious at the time, she took it home.

Now, when it rolled off the couch, Miss Adams started to rescue it, but refrained, remembering that three competent planets had guaranteed the puppy's well-being.

"Certainly I make mistakes," she finally answered as the griffon clumsily re-established its long body on its short legs.

In this *New Yorker* profile from 1928, we find the dog at the office with Adams. Evangeline also mentioned her in a letter from Germany:

The little dog was such a comfort on the voyage, and everybody has already fallen in love with her... This little Belgium Griffon was born February 8 (my birthday) 1927, and is the dearest little thing, only weighing 3¾ pounds. We have named her Sunaqua – my cable address – as her Sun is in Aquarius. She already loves Mr. Jordan and is devotion itself to me. She was no trouble on the boat.

Evangeline loved her many pets. She felt that people with strong Neptunes, as she had, needed to feel needed. Another dog, Sonnie, who was fifteen years old, had died shortly before of heart trouble and was buried on Adams' Westchester property.

Like Evangeline, Sunaqua had both Venus and Jupiter in Pisces, so they shared an even closer astrological bond than the same birthday! And Sunaqua's Saturn was only a few degrees from Evangeline's Saturn. The three planets that "guaranteed the puppy's well-being" were no doubt the Moon exalted in Taurus, Venus exalted in Pisces, and Jupiter dignified in Pisces.

George E. Jordan, Jr. was living in New Hampshire in July of 1958 when he had Evangeline's remains disinterred and moved to Connecticut. At around the same time, he seems to have sold Evangeline's library of astrology books.

Frank McDonough, a New Jersey businessman, read *The Bowl of Heaven* in the late fifties and became obsessed with finding Evangeline's library. After searching used bookstores in Boston and New York for three years, he finally found her collection of books. Included were many old and rare volumes such as an original copy of *Christian Astrology* by famed seventeenth century astrologer William Lilly.

His daughter, later the astrologer Margot Mason, became immediately attracted to the books when she came to visit her parents. She believed she was the reincarnation of Adams (she had been born about four years after Evangeline's death). Margot's mother concurred in *Here and Hereafter*, since she'd gone to the hospital on four false alarms and the baby was born a month late:

I have since wondered whether she delayed her birth until the exact time when she could have the horoscope which would coincide with that of Evangeline Adams. (Montgomery p. 142)

Mason felt that she and Adams had some close astrological connections:

"Her Sun is on my seventh house of partnerships," Margot explains. "Her Moon is in conjunction with my Sun and Ascendant. This always causes an unbreakable bond between two people. Attachments between Venus and Saturn in two horoscopes cause an everlasting friendship. Miss Adams' Venus is exactly 'on' my Saturn, the same degree and sign, in my eighth house – of death! In other words, this bond came after death." (Montgomery p. 141)

With Saturn in Pisces in her eighth house, Mason's parents provided the resources for her to move back home and spend much time studying the books in Evangeline's library. She eventually wrote about the value of astrology in raising children, a topic Evangeline had held dear. Mason said,

It was as if I were taking a refresher course, because I auto-matically knew the answers. No other kind of learning had ever come this easily to me. (Montgomery p. 143)

She digested much of the library within three years. Margot Mason died in 1976, a victim of cancer at the age of 40.

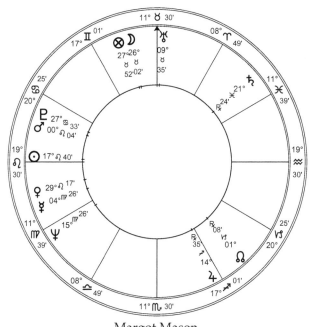

Margot Mason
August 10, 1936 5:21 AM MST
Denver, CO 39N45 104W59
Source: Ruth Montgomery's *Here and Hereafter*, p. 142.

In 1977, Norman Winski, a Chicago Board Options Exchange floor trader, financial consultant and astrologer, learned about Evangeline Adams, her reputation as an advisor to J.P. Morgan, and her forecast of the 1929 stock market crash. Norman thought that if he could find Evangeline's library or papers, perhaps he could learn some stock market forecasting techniques. Coincidentally, he happened upon some old papers several months later and came across an astrology newsletter with an article written by Margot Mason, mentioning Evangeline Adams' library.

Winski discovered that Margot had died the previous year, and Margot's parents sold the books to Norman. It's intriguing to notice that, as before, someone searched for the books just as they became available.

After his purchase, Winski met Adams' great-niece, Evangeline Adams Curry Elmore, who had all the family memorabilia. A few years later, upon Mrs. Elmore's death, her husband gave Winski all of the Adams papers. Some items of note are a *bas-relief* of Evangeline Adams that she had sent to her niece Gertrude in 1931, and Evangeline's letters. The library and other information are still with Norman in his home in Naples, Florida.

Norman Winski has yet another horoscope with an emphasis on Aquarius and Pisces, as we've found so often in Evangeline's associates. Like Evangeline, the Sun in Aquarius is configured with Pluto, and Venus and Jupiter are both in Pisces. Uranus is close to the same degree in Cancer as in Evangeline's chart. Evangeline's Midheaven falls right on Norman's Ascendant.

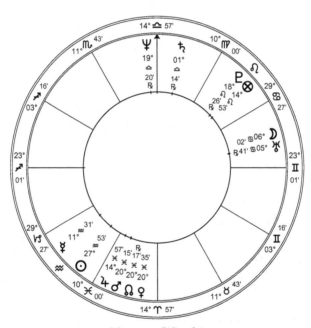

Norman Winski
February 17, 1951 2:55 AM CST
Frankfort, IN 40N16 86W30
Source: Winski, citing his birth certificate.

Part II: What Evangeline Knew

3. Adams' Famous Fortune-Telling Trial

Evangeline's trial for fortune-telling in 1914 was a pivotal event in her career. She was exonerated and thus gained much exposure and credibility as a result. Her fame was insured. The trial is one of the main reasons Evangeline is remembered today, as the magistrate's decision set a legal precedent in New York City.

But from the point of view of the astrologer who wants to discover the "real" Evangeline Adams, the trial transcript may be more valuable. Nowhere else do we ever hear Evangeline live and uncensored. Since no audio recordings of her radio show and very few of her personal letters survive, the court reporter's transcript is the closest we can come to hearing the actual woman in action.

With her Saturn in Sagittarius in the ninth house squaring Mercury, Evangeline had several run-ins with the law. She was first arrested on January 12, 1911, with a hearing on January 16. The case was dismissed. Her arrest on May 14, 1914 and examination on May 19 led to her much publicized fortune-telling trial. Adams' final arrest came on January 24, 1923; this case was also dismissed. None of these arrests were the result of client complaints: all came about through police sting operations in which psychics and palmists were also arrested.

Louis MacNeice quoted Adams' student Iris Vorel as saying in her *Astrologer's Handbook* that Evangeline said, "I will always triumph over my enemies!" (MacNeice p. 198) Adams' Ascendant ruler, Jupiter, placed in one of its own signs, is stronger than the ruler of her seventh house of open enemies, Mercury, in detriment in Pisces.

Transiting Jupiter was at 11° Scorpio at the time of the first arrest, squaring Evangeline's Mars but forming a grand trine with natal Jupiter and Uranus. She gained much publicity for this arrest, as she had done twelve years earlier at the time she had claimed to predict the famous Windsor Hotel fire, with Jupiter near the same position. On the third arrest twelve years later, Jupiter was at 16½° Scorpio, squaring her Sun but still trine Jupiter, while approaching a trine to natal Venus. For the most famous arrest however, Jupiter was at 21°

Aquarius, just past conjoining Evangeline's Sun and opposing her Moon, while Saturn in Gemini trined her Sun. Uranus stationed in conjunction with her Mars and sextiled first house Neptune.

The trial was postponed until December 11, 1914, presumably for Adams' attorney to learn enough astrology to prepare for the trial. But were there astrological reasons? While Saturn was close to 18° Gemini on May 14, trining Adams' Sun from the third house, by December it would be at 29 Gemini 40, conjunct her end-of-the-matter fourth house cusp and just a degree away from favorably trining Evangeline's natal Mercury, ruler of her seventh house of open enemies. Jupiter at the time of the arrest was closely opposed to Evangeline's Moon. While it would advance and retrograde during the next several months, on the day of the trial it was at 18 and a half Aquarius, within about a half a degree of conjoining Evangeline's Sun and thus implying victory. As she said in her *Guide for 1933*:

> This is a constructive and very beneficial vibration which makes for harmony with both yourself and others. Hence, your relations with other people and your influence over them is likely to be both pleasant and fortunate. (*1933* p. 268)

The *New York World* quoted Adams as saying that her planets were in such an "auspicious position" that she felt she would win even if she had to take the case to the Supreme Court.

Adams consistently turned her legal problems to her own advantage. Her natal Saturn, as well as the Midheaven and Ascendant, are all disposed by Jupiter, dignified in its traditional rulership of Pisces. Using traditional rulerships we also find it to be the final dispositor of the chart. This protected Adams throughout her life.

The following excerpts from the trial of December 11, 1914 are taken from Walter Coleman's *Astrology and the Law*. The original text appears in the *New York Criminal Reports*, Volume XXXII. Note that this is not a complete transcript – only Magistrate Freschi's summary with a partial transcription was included. I've edited the report a bit for clarity, as much of the original is rambling and repetitious. I have also added some explanatory notes in italics.

The only witness for the prosecution is Mrs. Adele D. Priess, who is attached to the Detective Bureau of the New York Police. She testified that on May 13, 1914, she visited the defendant at her studio located at Carnegie Hall, in the City and County of New York, and there had her horoscope "read" by the defendant.

The complainant claims that all she can remember of her conversation with the defendant is as follows:

"There was a sheet of paper before her with a circle described on it, divided into sections. The defendant referred to a book, and occasionally wrote on the paper. The defendant said 'Now place your hands on the table, palms down. Place them very flat,' which I did. The defendant said, 'Your hands show that you have got practical common sense. You should not go to people for advice. You should follow out your own ideas, and carry out your plans as you make them at first. The left hand tells of your early life and the right hand of your later life. You are going to be more successful and have more magnetism in later life than in earlier life. This is shown by the third finger of your right hand being longer than the third finger of your left hand.'

'There is a new epoch opening for you. If you were a young girl, I should say that you were going to have a violent love affair, but I don't know if you are free.' I said, 'I have been divorced a number of years.' She said, 'Then I should say that you are going to meet a man for whom you might form an attachment, but I should be very careful about marrying him in case his circumstances should be such that he could not get along without your help. I was right in selecting midnight as about the time of your birth because Mars was in the marriage sign, which shows separation. Let me see the palm of your hand.' I turned my hand over. The defendant said 'I see two marriages in your hand.'

'You are very optimistic. You might be depressed for a little while but that passes over. You are too unselfish for your own good. People are apt to impose upon you. During the years 1907 and 1908 were you very unhappy?' I replied 'Yes.' The defendant said 'You will never again be as unhappy as you were then. Now, are there any young people about you?' I said 'Yes, I have two daughters and a son.'

During 1908, Saturn was roughly conjunct Priess' Moon; and Neptune, passing from 11° to 17° Cancer opposed her Mercury from 1907 to 1908.

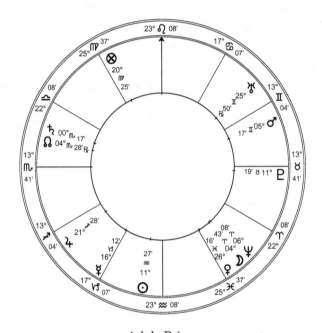

Adele Priess
January 31, 1865 New York, NY 40N43 74W00
Source: Court transcript includes data with an Ascendant
rectified by sign by Evangeline.

The defendant said 'Is your elder daughter married?' I said 'No.' The defendant said 'What is the date of her birth?' I said 'October 12, 1889, at eleven a.m.' The defendant took a fresh piece of paper, on which there was a circle described, as I described before, and consulted a book, and wrote on the paper. The defendant said, 'Your daughter is going to have a very eventful life. She will marry the first man to whom she becomes engaged. Do you know that she has great talent? Does she trim hats and sew?' I said 'No, she does not, neither has she great talent. She is lacking in ambition. What you say belongs more to the younger girl.' The defendant said 'You do not understand your daughter. Sometimes she is obstinate.'

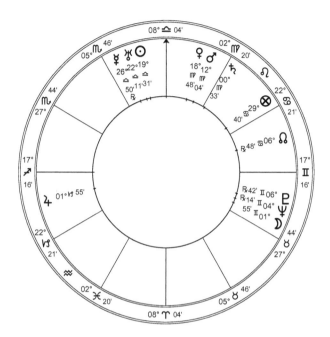

Adele's Elder Daughter
October 12, 1889   11:00 AM EST
New York, NY   40N43   74W00
Source: Court report provides the data.

Evangeline used a technique taught by Dr. Smith and Dr. Broughton to describe the marriage partner (see pages 96-97). Priess recollects Adams' judgment wrongly – see Adams' testimony, which follows.

'Tell me the date of the younger girl's birth.' I said, 'April 16, 1894, at two o'clock p.m.' The defendant said 'Your daughter is very ambitious; she was born when Saturn was rising. She sometimes gets discouraged, but that soon passes over just like a wet blanket. Tell me what is her occupation?' I said, 'My daughter attends high school. I should like her to become a teacher, but she is thinking of opening a dancing studio with another young lady in the fall.' The defendant said 'I should not advise her to do that, to open a studio in the fall.

Perhaps next year would be better. Do you know the date of the other young lady's birth?' I said 'No.' The defendant said 'I should not spend so much money; put up so much money. If I knew the date of this other young lady's birth, I could give her more advice. Your younger daughter will marry well, but your elder daughter will make a far better marriage than the younger one.'

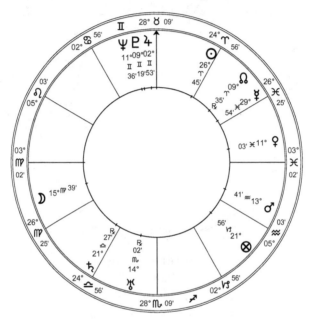

Adele's Younger Daughter
April 16, 1894 2:00 PM EST
New York, NY 40N43 74W00
Source: Court report provides the data.

Neptune in Cancer was within orb of squaring the young lady's Aries Sun that fall, retrograding back towards the exact square the following year. As Adams said in her Guide for 1933, this aspect suggests that one,

Be sure any schemes which are brought to your attention are not visionary or irresponsible. Be equally sure of the integrity of any people with whom you form an association. (p. 258)

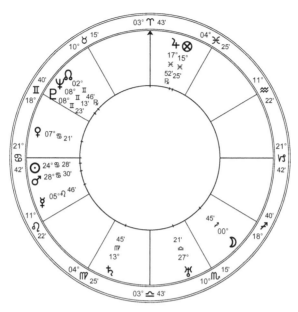

Adele's Son
July 17, 1891 4:30 AM EST
New York, NY 40N43 74W00
Source: Court report provides the data.

'What is the date of your son's birth?' I said, 'He was born July 17, 1891, at 4:30 a.m.' Then the defendant took a fresh piece of paper with a circle inscribed on it, and then consulted the book. The defendant said, 'Your son will be very successful. He makes friends very easily. He should be careful about his companions, as he is apt to be influenced by them. He should guard against dissipation. What is his occupation?' I said, 'My son attends college; he expects to graduate this year. He would like to take up a mining engineering course. I cannot afford to let him have it. He might take something in the electrical line.' She said 'Your son is very bright, but the work around bridges or water works I should not advise him to have anything to do with, going up in an airplane or around electricity where there is a high voltage, or have anything to do with automobile racing, for he might meet with an accident. Your son should be very careful for he will die as the result of an accident or die very suddenly just like that,' snapping the defendant's fingers.

Adams is obviously reading the afflictions of Neptune and particularly Uranus squaring the young man's first house Mars.

'You are going to be very much upset during July or August about one of your children, but things are going to be very bright for you.' I said to the defendant 'How much is that? Five dollars?' The defendant said 'Yes.' I thereupon paid the defendant. The defendant said 'Now if your daughter and her friend will come here some evening around five o'clock I will give them a reading for three dollars.'"

Transiting Saturn in Gemini would conjoin natal Uranus and square Venus in Priess' fifth house, suggesting difficulties with one of her children.

Following the detective's testimony, Evangeline Adams is allowed to give her account of the events in question. I have omitted the attorney's questions to make for easier reading.

"I asked her to be seated and asked her time of birth. She said 1865, January 31. I asked her if she could not give me the hour of her birth. She said no. Then I said 'It will be impossible for me to give you a correct or wholly satisfactory reading because all I can tell you is what I can tell any one who was born on that day!' I then said 'I am determined whether by your appearance –' I asked her to move her head so that I could see her profile. I studied her face for a moment like over this book, which gives the type of the twelve signs of the Zodiac. I decided there were two signs under which she might be born. I said 'You might have been born under Scorpio or Taurus.' I then said 'If you were born under Scorpio, you would be secretive and non-communicative. If under Taurus, you would be frank, outspoken and domestic.' She said, 'I am non-communicative.' I then looked up in that same book to see when Scorpio would rise. I found that at midnight, the sign of Scorpio would rise.

After I had the chart erected, I told her I got characteristics from the hand. I asked her to sit to the left of my desk, at a small table. I asked her to place her hands on that table, palms down. I glanced over the hand and told her many things about her nails. She should never take antikamnia, nor any coal tar products, because there was a tendency to suffer from poor elimination, and anything that depressed the heart would be bad for her.

Evangeline was still using palmistry as an integral part of her work in 1914. After the trial, however, she would publicly espouse only astrology. Later reports of subsequent readings confirm that she concentrated on astrology as the years went on, perhaps because it was easier to legitimize than palmistry.

I said that the third finger in palmistry is said to rule, the 'Sun finger' as we say. That it being long indicates that she had quite strong impressions, the kind of impressions that the Wall Street men call 'hunches,' and if she would go by these 'hunches' without talking them over with anyone that she might be fortunate in speculation. I also said that the left hand indicated the natural tendencies, was supposed to rule until 28, and the right hand the balance of life, and that as this third finger was longer on the right hand the indications were that the last half of her life should be more fortunate than the earlier half. I think at the same time, I thought the last half should be more happy, more fortunate, she would be more magnetic because of this third finger.

I pursued my usual method. I took up Mercury, which was in the sign Capricorn, and that gave her a tendency to have great periods of depression. She would feel at times as if a wet blanket had been thrown over her feelings, and then would disappear without apparently any reason. One of the things that I laid a great deal of stress upon was the position of her moon. The moon was in conjunction with the planet Neptune. I asked her what happened to her mother, if there was any strange fatality connected with her mother's life. It took her a long time before she would commit herself. At last she said, 'Yes, my mother was shot.' I read it right in the chart,

'Mother was shot but didn't die until eight years later.' Right before her I read that in the chart.

I spoke of the fact that the planet Uranus during this year would be in conjunction with the sun, which occurs only once in eighty-four years, and that it was also an epoch-making period. That this was the planet that brought about changes, a great deal of development in the character, etc., and that if she were a young girl it might have caused her to have an opportunity to marry. That in this case it might bring someone into her life who would bring some new interest or something of a philosophic or scientific character to her. I explained that Herschel is in conjunction with her sun this year, and that that always indicated new vibrations, new conditions.

It's fascinating to notice that Uranus was stationing in exact conjunction with Detective Priess' Sun on the day of the interview, May 13, 1914; she was, after all, consulting an astrologer!

I talked for an hour. I don't know that this is all I stated about her chart, but I do remember that I asked her if there were any other people about whom she might like to ask. She gave me the date of the daughter. I told her that the sun was unfriendly to Hershel and that that indicated that she would not marry or be likely to marry the first man to whom she was engaged, that she must be careful about her friendships, as it indicated temptations. I told her that the position of Jupiter was in Capricorn, and that I had found many successful dressmakers and milliners that had that sign and that she ought to have ability in that direction.

Evangeline elsewhere says her usual appointments were half an hour. Detective Priess also testified that the appointment lasted about 35 minutes. Mentioning an hour seems to be an example of Evangeline's "creative remembering" – whether intentional or not.

She then gave the date of another daughter. I do recall that she told me that she was thinking of starting a dancing school this fall. Saturn was rising and that indicated that she was ambitious but lacking in confidence, or might be at times lacking in confidence, I thought was the sum of it. I said that next year she was going to have better planetary conditions, and if she still thought of doing it the chances were more favorable of meeting with success. I explained the opposition of Mercury indicated that she would have periods of depression and that it was similar to a wet blanket.

Adams loosely describes Saturn in Libra as "rising" and "about to come up" since the young woman had Virgo rising. She did not draw up a full chart, so perhaps "the opposition of Mercury" refers generally to the Moon or Ascendant. Adams tells us in The Bowl of Heaven *that she worked very quickly when drawing up charts, as she seems to do here. She included a 35-page table of Ascendants in her book,* Astrology Your Place in the Sun, *and perhaps she had already prepared such a table for herself for daily use with clients.*

She then gave me the date of her son's birth. I said emphatically it was a very unusual horoscope. I know certain planets were in certain aspects, which indicated danger of an accidental death and that I advised him not to work where there was high voltage. I did tell her he had ability along electrical lines, but that he ought not to work in high voltage because of this aspect in his horoscope, which indicated danger of accidents and even accidental death.

Adams is probably reading Uranus as the ruler of the Aquarian eighth house in the son's chart, although she still at times refers to it as "Hershel."

I explain in the beginning I simply give what is shown by the stars. If I read for a client I always say 'This is indicated' and I always explain that no astrologer can conscientiously say that any one thing will happen. Sometimes a lady will say 'Will I be married in 1914?' I say, 'I don't know whether you will or not. I think you have an opportunity to be but whether you will I can't tell. Astrology does not indicate you are going to be haled to the altar.' I am very careful to say what will occur, because I don't know. In fact, I simply say, 'This is likely to be, guard against it, if it is bad. If it is good, make the most of it.' There is no client that comes to me that does not realize they are simply getting my ideas of what the planet will do or so far as the planet indicates. They draw their own deductions. They know so much about astrology. They don't know the mathematical end of it.

That is all I ever do. I am very careful to do it. I am careful to do it not because I think the law is involved, but because I do not want any responsibility. I do not want to feel that I have anything to do with it. I say I have nothing to do with it, I simply read the signs. An astrologist feels a great deal of responsibility and tries to make it plain. Human nature is very funny."

Magistrate Freschi concluded with some very favorable words about Evangeline:

Counsel contends that the defendant did not pretend to foretell any event, that all that occurred was an attempt on her part to explain the positions of the planets and read their indications without any assurance by the defendant that such reading was a prognostication of future events.

There is no claim here that the defendant was garbed in special garments or that there was any air of mysticism about the place; it was a simple apartment with library furniture without signs of any kind in or about the studio, except to indicate that it was the office of the defendant.

Several works on modern astrology as well as very old books on the subject were produced in court. These were used by the defendant while testifying and in the construction of the horoscope in a supposed case. In the reading of the horoscope the defendant went through an absolutely mechanical, mathematical process to get at her conclusions. She claims that astrology never makes a mistake and that if the figures are correct, the information given is correct.

Evangeline would later say that the judge allowed her to read the chart of his son, Joseph. While it does not appear in this account, the "supposed case" Freschi refers to may be that of his son. The only astrology book explicitly mentioned in the transcript is Richard Garnett's work, which Evangeline claimed to be "among the best authorities." It included a section on accidental death.

The defendant raises astrology to the dignity of an exact science – one of vibration, and she claims that all the planets represent different forces of the universe.

The sincerity of the defendant's determination upon the opinion of her work from her own perceptions and a study of authorities cannot be questioned. She certainly does seem to have a thorough knowledge of the subject. And in this, she claims no faculty of foretelling by supernatural or magical means that which is future, or of discovering that which is hidden or obscure; but she does claim that nature is to be interpreted by the influences that surround it.

The statute in question is peculiarly worded. "Pretend to tell fortunes" are to be considered. This law was designed to prohibit persons who make pretense or make believe to tell fortunes. A deception or concealment of the truth is essential in each case. It is really a certain degree of quackery practiced to the detriment of the community, in general, that is made unlawful by this statute.

When the defendant prepared her horoscope of the complainant and got the relative position of the planets at the time of her birth, basing this horoscope on the well-known and fixed science of astronomy, she violated no law. Her explanation of the relative positions of the planets constituted no violation of law. For the palmist to tell that a certain line in the palm of the hand is the "life line" or the "head line" or the "heart line" has never been held, as far as I know, a violation of this law now under consideration, but it has been held to constitute one a disorderly person, within the meaning of this statute, to say that the life of a certain individual will be long or short.

Every fortune-teller is a violator of the law; but every astrologer is not a fortune-teller. I believe that there is a line of distinction between the person who pretends to be able to read the future and tell with positiveness what will or shall happen; and the one who merely reads a sign as indicating what ought to happen but is particular to make it plain that he is not attempting to predict future events. The former is a charlatan, an oppressor and an imposter; the latter is surely not a fortune-teller as he is commonly understood.

4. An Astrologer's Toolkit

Electional and Event Charts

No one can say for certain just how much time and trouble Evangeline Adams took with any of the following charts: they simply represent dates and times which have been confirmed by documentation. Yet as a practicing astrologer as well as someone who believed in her gospel wholeheartedly, Evangeline would have enjoyed electing charts for her own benefit. Aleister Crowley has told us in "How Horoscopes are Faked" that,

> She talks astrology day and night. She dreams of it. She sets a horoscope for her vast family of cats and dogs, and is scared out of her life when some planet threatens her horoscope.

We can assume Adams was thus cautious with important events in her life and elected astrological times for them. Her own astrology books were designed primarily for beginners, and she never discussed Electional astrology. But she had a huge consulting business and regularly elected dates for clients, particularly surgical dates. The following charts can give us an idea of the techniques Adams used. But there is also evidence of practicality: life must go on, regardless of whether or not an ideal time presents itself! Finally, however, some of these charts may simply represent inceptions, and not actual elections – there's no way to know for sure.

Evangeline appears to have utilized essential dignities, a concept that has currently fallen into disuse (see Appendix II for the dignities Dr. Broughton used). The Sun is at its best in its ruling sign of Leo, the Moon quite strong in its exaltation of Taurus, and so on. These dignities and debilities have been with us since Babylonian times.

Adams apparently had no fear of the malefics, which figure prominently in her own chart. Remember, too, that Pluto was discovered in 1930, so ephemerides of its placement would not have been available for use in any of these elections.

We don't have many timed charts chosen by Evangeline herself, so let's first look at one elected by her teacher, Catherine Thompson. Thompson organized the Boston branch of the Baconian Society of America and was its secretary. This group believed that Francis Bacon was the true Shakespeare.

Thompson studied with Dr. Luke D. Broughton, and his influence can also be seen on Adams' work. Dr. Broughton's rules for electing a new business enterprise are as follows:

> First, let the Sun or Moon be in their dignities or at least not afflicted by Saturn, Mars or Uranus. Second, let Jupiter be in the Ascendant and the Sun in the Midheaven if possible. Third, let the seventh and second houses be strong and fortunate, for one signifies money and the other counsels for the native's assistance; for if these houses are afflicted it shows great damage to the native. Let Jupiter and Venus be strong if possible, and in good aspect in the election horoscope. (Broughton p. 288)

In this chart, the Sun is not afflicted, and favorably sextiles Mars and trines the Moon. The Moon is dignified in Cancer and prominently placed in the tenth house. (Pluto was unknown in 1926.) Both the second and seventh houses are ruled by an angular Mars in its exaltation in Capricorn, also strongly placed on the IC. Venus rules and trines the Ascendant, and if not dignified, is closely conjunct Jupiter in the fifth house. Jupiter also rules the third house of writing, the topic of interest itself.

The group was successful. Clemens says that many Bostonians took a great interest in the group and were willing to donate large sums of money to the society. But the national president, the Boston president and finally Thompson herself had all passed away by 1934, so the society existed for less than eight years. Mars in Capricorn at the IC disposits much of the chart and opposes the Moon and Pluto, ultimately sending the group's instigators and the enterprise itself to the grave.

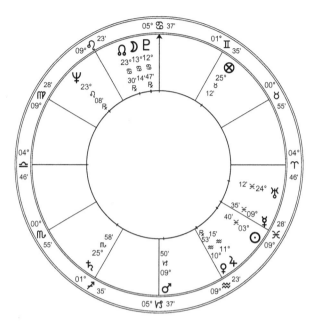

Boston Chapter of the Bacon Society Founded
February 22, 1926 8:00 PM EST
Boston, MA 42N22 71W04
Source: *The Autobiography of Marie Louise Clemens*
provides the date and time on p. 273.

While Evangeline Adams was the most popular astrologer in the country in 1923, her relationships had not been as successful. She had broken off an early engagement, scandalizing her family in the process. Later, the famous sculptor Franklin Simmons proposed marriage, but he was nearly thirty years Evangeline's senior and wanted her to stop working which made him unsuitable (although the age difference doesn't seem to have bothered Evangeline herself). Adams remained single and dedicated herself to her work.

Evangeline was nearly 53 when she met her future husband, George E. Jordan, Jr. The marriage must have been a serious decision, as it did not take place for over two years. Adams had Virgo on the seventh house cusp, with its ruler, Mercury, placed in Pisces in the twelfth house. She had probably been fantasizing about the ideal partnership for years. But Mercury was in square to Saturn, her most elevated planet, and her marriage had been delayed.

Transiting Saturn opposed Evangeline's natal Venus from the seventh house cusp in 1921, when she first met George Jordan. It would continue through this house for the next three years, putting a greater emphasis on both partnership and business. Saturn through the seventh is quite different in its influence than Saturn in the seventh house natally. While it may end existing relationships, it is usually the case that these were somehow lacking to begin with, or have become responsibilities we no longer wish to embrace. Important events and decisions involving significant partnerships often occur during Saturn's transit of the seventh house, especially when it aspects other planets. Individuals become more serious about relationships during these times, and are no longer looking for fun, but tend toward settling down. It seems this was the case with Evangeline as well.

Evangeline Adams had already been studying astrology for nearly 35 years, and was in professional practice for over 25. She was an expert astrologer and certainly took some time to choose a wedding date. With her Mercury square Saturn relating particularly to marriage, Adams would have worried and fussed over the details of this chart, hoping to make the most of the relationship.

Evangeline was married in New York City on April 12, 1923, according to her marriage certificate. Church records confirm this date, and give us a time of 2:45 p.m.

While Electional charts must stand on their own, they should ideally be compatible with the native's birth chart, too. Virgo rises in the wedding chart, which is the same sign Evangeline has on her seventh house cusp. There are also three planets in Pisces, which reflect the Pisces emphasis in Adams' birth chart.

Evangeline had Jupiter in its traditional rulership of Pisces, and she always felt this was one of the best things in her chart. So it's no surprise to see that the wedding day and time highlight Jupiter. The three Pisces planets in the wedding chart all trine Jupiter in Scorpio,

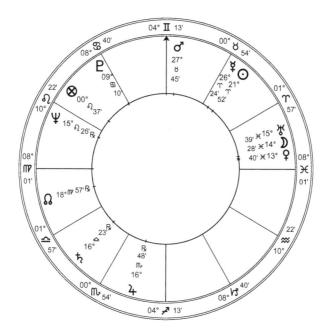

Adams' Wedding
April 12, 1923 2:45 PM EST
New York, NY 40N43 74W00
Source: Marriage certificate for date; church records for time.

forming a grand trine with Adams' natal Jupiter-Uranus trine. (Pluto in Cancer creates a grand trine in the election chart, but hadn't yet been discovered. A lucky break for Evangeline!) Adams chose a Thursday for the ceremony, which is the day ruled by Jupiter. And the time gives us a Jupiter hour as well.

Those with experience in choosing elections will realize at once how very difficult it is to find suitable dates. Even if we have no practical limitations, planetary interactions typically offer mixed influences. It was no mean feat to find a Jupiter day, Jupiter hour, and trines from Jupiter that support the bride's natal chart and event Moon and Venus at the same time – try it and see. Yet, in addition, this chart has many other things to recommend it.

In most marriages of the time, the Ascendant represented the man (the person initiating the proposal) and the Descendant the woman. Dr. Luke D. Broughton in his book *Elements of Astrology* says that "if the fortunate planets are in the seventh house, the woman receives the most advantage by marriage." (p. 289) With the Moon and Venus in the seventh house trine Jupiter, it's crystal clear who this chart was chosen for!

Evangeline utilized essential dignities in her selection. In the wedding chart we find the Sun in Aries, Venus in Pisces and Saturn in Libra, all in the signs of their exaltations. Yet beyond this, Venus is in the term of Venus, and both the Moon and Venus are in the face of Jupiter. The Ascendant and Jupiter are in the term of Venus. What more could one ask for?

Mars is the only planet which has no dignity; it's placed in Taurus, the sign of its detriment. (See Appendix II on page 188 for Broughton's Essential Dignities table.) Only Jupiter is retrograde.

As one would expect for a wedding chart, the Moon is emphasized over the Sun through its angular placement. The Sun opposite Saturn takes us by surprise, but both planets are placed in the signs of their exaltation, and so are better able to stand up to a stressful aspect. In addition, Adams felt that one of the best influences on Saturn was the Sun, as it illuminated it. Certainly, with so much water in this chart, it benefits from Saturn's ballast as well. Although wide, Mercury is drawn into this pattern, too. But Adams always felt that Mercury could benefit from the stabilizing force of Saturn. And once again, this aspect is reminiscent of Evangeline's own chart, with its Mercury square Saturn hooked in with the seventh house.

Evangeline Adams was an Aquarian and also had Uranus in the fourth house. She would not be someone to choose typical placements and aspects. The chart would be uniquely her own. Most obvious are the trines between the Pisces planets and Jupiter in Scorpio. We can well understand the Moon and Venus in Pisces in the seventh – quite sentimental, as her own Venus in Pisces would like. Yet this pattern involves Uranus as well, with the Moon approaching a close conjunction with Uranus. And in the seventh house, no less! This is rather shocking as it is certainly not a stable indication for marriage. Yet the choice does reflect Evangeline's strongly Aquarian nature. If the seventh house describes her, we see she is a Uranian Piscean, which is quite true. Her relationship with her husband must have been an unusual one.

The strongest pattern in the wedding chart is a yod, made up of the Moon, Venus, and Uranus all conjunct, with quincunxes to both Saturn and Neptune. One can only wonder at this odd choice, and yet it is a powerful combination, stressing idealism, adaptability and independence. The Saturn-Neptune sextile unites high hopes with realism. The only square in the chart is Jupiter with Neptune, once again emphasizing idealism and spirituality. If Evangeline had high expectations for the marriage, she was certainly willing to bet on them.

This chart is also notable for the presence of minor aspects. The Sun and to a lesser extent Mercury, oppose Saturn; Mars widely opposes Jupiter. Yet Saturn semi-sextiles Jupiter and Mars semi-sextiles Mercury, creating a mini mystic rectangle. There are quintiles between the Moon-Uranus conjunction and Mars, as well as between Mercury and Pluto (was the latter a coincidence or just plain luck?).

But what, in fact, was this relationship all about? The strong Pisces placements and many Neptune aspects indicate Adams' love, as well as her optimism for the union. The presence of Mars in Taurus ruling the eighth house widely opposed to Jupiter in Scorpio may point toward sensuality, particularly as Mars is so close to the Midheaven. The Ascendant ruler Mercury along with the Sun in the eighth house implies an emphasis on sexuality, and it's been suggested that Jordan was such a disagreeable man that Evangeline wanted him just for sex!

Saturn's opposition to the Sun should indicate more practical considerations, and this marriage was as much a business partnership as a personal one. Jordan joined with his wife to turn her consulting business into a vast astrological enterprise. During the marriage Adams wrote her books, secured her fame through publicity and broadcasting, and expanded her business with written reports reaching countless thousands across the country. The emphasis on Jupiter in the wedding chart paid off. But is this a chart that stresses business or sex? Work or pleasure? Perhaps a little of both. The marriage lasted only nine and a half years, ending in Adams' death.

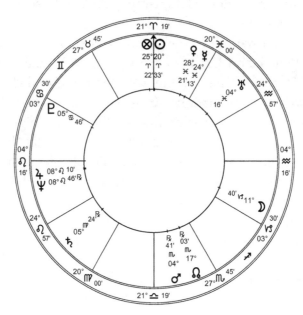

Gertrude Adams' Wedding
April 10, 1920 Decatur, Illinois 39N50 88W57
Source: Marriage certificate for date; noon chart.

Evangeline Adams never had any children and remained distant from most of her relatives. Yet her niece, Gertrude, was close to her. Gertrude's Moon in Aquarius mirrored her aunt's Sun, and they shared the placement of Jupiter in Pisces (see p. 76). When Gertrude got married, we can only assume that Aunt Evangeline had a hand in selecting her wedding date as well. The date is from Gertrude's marriage certificate, but as no time is available, I have cast a noon chart. Here we see similar placements of the Sun in Aries and Venus in Pisces, both exalted. The square between Mars and Jupiter-Neptune is modified by Mars' exalted placement in Scorpio, and Jupiter in the sign of Leo, one of its triplicities. When we include Pluto, a mystic rectangle is formed along with the Moon,

Saturn and Uranus. Evangeline almost seems to have an intuitive feel for utilizing the then unknown Pluto! It is unfortunate that we don't have a time for this chart, but it does confirm Evangeline Adams' use of the essential dignities.

The only surprise in Gertrude's wedding chart is the Moon's placement in Capricorn, the sign of its detriment. Yet the Moon is also in one of its triplicities in Capricorn, since it is an earth sign. The Moon is very important in a wedding election, as it determines the emotional tenor of the union. But Gertrude was 28 at the time of her marriage, and was nearing her Saturn return. She also has the Sun squaring Saturn in her birth chart, so the Capricorn Moon does reflect her age and character. If not warm, it certainly emphasizes stability and restraint. Gertrude's husband Claude Curry, (born on December 9, 1889, according to his death certificate), had the Sun, Mercury and Venus all in Sagittarius, with the Moon in a probable T-square with Mars and Uranus. He could use some restraint! And he was thirty at the time of their wedding as well.

Unfortunately, when we compare the Electional placements with Gertrude's chart, we don't get a harmonious picture. The transiting Saturn-Uranus opposition squared her Sun, Neptune and Pluto in Gemini, and pulled in the square from her natal Saturn in Virgo. Mars in Scorpio opposed her Venus in Taurus. We get the impression that she might have rushed into the marriage, which her Mars trine Uranus and husband's Mars conjunct Uranus tended to do. But the choice of the Capricorn Moon smoothes things out by trining and sextiling the Saturn-Uranus opposition and sextiling Mars in the election and Venus in the natal. The one square in the election, between Mars and Jupiter conjunct Neptune, is also opened out somewhat when we combine it with Gertrude's birth chart. Jupiter and Neptune are both just past squaring Venus and are closer to sextiling the Gemini planets. The wedding Mars does oppose natal Venus, but it sextiles her Saturn as well, and its placement in its own sign of Scorpio keeps it from being as malefic as it could be.

This marriage lasted twenty years, ending in the husband's death at the age of 51. The couple had three children, including a boy who died of heart disease at the age of sixteen. Claude lost his job during the depression, but Aunt Evangeline helped them through. A typical Sagittarian male, Claude probably had interests outside the family. Adams scolded Gertrude in a 1932 letter,

If you find that he is spending one penny on anyone but his family... that will be the finish and I shall do everything to help you get free of him.

Some of these difficult events are perhaps hinted at in the Moon's opposition to Pluto and Mars' square to Neptune in the wedding chart. These two wedding charts make a fascinating study, as they are the best examples we have of how Evangeline Adams used Electional astrology.

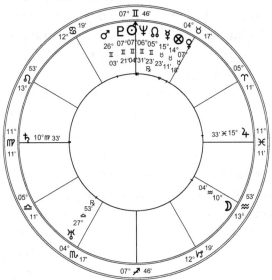

Helen Gertrude Adams
May 28, 1891 Chicago, IL 41N51 87W39
Source: Birth Certificate; noon chart.

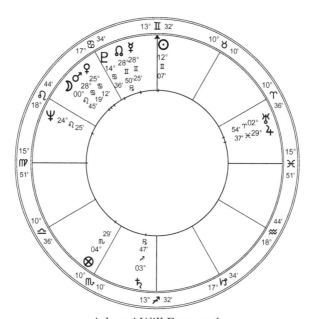

Adams' Will Executed
June 3, 1927 New York, NY 40N43 74W00
Source: NYC Surrogates Court Records; time is speculative.

The chart for the day Evangeline drew up her will is simplicity itself. A grand trine made up of Moon, Venus, Mars, Jupiter, Saturn, and Uranus dominated. Mercury is placed in Gemini for this important legal document, although interestingly it squares the Jupiter-Uranus conjunction. The stress is again mitigated, however, by Jupiter and Mercury both dignified by sign.

We once again have a wide opposition between the Sun and Saturn. Adams did feel that the Sun helped to "illuminate" Saturn, and in this case, the sign placements describe the event: Gemini for the document itself and Sagittarius for the legal factors involved. And Sun-Saturn symbolizes planning for death in the midst of life.

Evangeline was experiencing her second Saturn return that year, and naturally thinking about the future. She left most of her estate to her husband, with generous bequests to her niece Gertrude and three assistants who had loyally served her over the years.

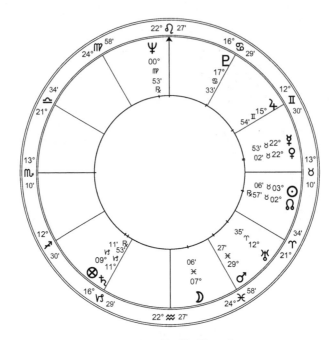

Adams' First Radio Broadcast
April 23, 1930 7:30 PM EST
New York, NY 40N43 74W00
Source: *New York Times* of November 11, 1932.

Perhaps Adams' first radio broadcast was simply an event, or inception chart, since we don't know how much control she had over scheduling. However, it's worthwhile studying it in any case, since the show was quite successful. The show premiered on a Wednesday, which is ruled by Mercury, the planet of communications. The Moon in Pisces reflects her own planetary emphasis and adds a transcendental glow. Both Venus and Saturn are dignified in their own signs, and Venus is accentuated by its angular placement in the seventh house, adding to the solid public appeal. Only Jupiter is in the sign of its detriment, but in the eighth house it is not as powerful. The Moon, Mercury, Venus and Neptune all angular seem ideal for a venture that would reach a vast number of people.

Within the first three months Evangeline Adams hosted her fifteen minute, twice weekly radio show, she reported receiving 150,000 letters from listeners. The next year, as the show grew to three times a week, she received approximately 4,000 letters a day. These must be relatively accurate figures, as the responses were due largely to an offer for a free horoscope if one sent in box tops from the sponsor's toothpaste! *Radio Round-Ups* reported that "Your Stars" received more fan mail than any other program in 1931, and said that Adams "took the country by storm." (MacDonald p. 44)

The main pattern in this chart is a kite, made up of a grand trine of Sun, Saturn and Neptune with sextiles and an opposition from the Moon. The Sun-Saturn trine attests to the business side of the broadcast, as do Sun, Mercury and Venus all in Taurus. Adams was promoting herself as well as the toothpaste.

Evangeline enjoyed a nationwide hookup of 44 stations, an impressive number at a time when radio was still in its infancy. The Scorpio Ascendant points toward the ability to reach the masses and the metaphysical nature of the topic discussed. If we include Pluto, there is a loose grand trine formed with the Ascendant and the Moon as well. Ascendant ruler Mars sextiles the seventh house planets and is in its triplicity in Pisces. While most of us today would consider Mars not at its best in this sign, it, too, puts the emphasis on reaching a wide, almost limitless, audience. The Moon in Pisces in the fourth and its opposition to Neptune in the tenth are similar influences.

The only real problem lies in the square from Saturn to Uranus, a particularly difficult aspect (of course Pluto creates a T-square). Yet there is something very like Saturn square Uranus in taking such a traditional topic to the airwaves The show, however, lasted only a little over a year. Saturn is placed in its own sign, moderating its malefic force. We find it transiting Evangeline's tenth house, stationary in motion, and sextiling her ruler, Jupiter. Although Saturn has technically just turned retrograde, all other planets are direct. Transiting Uranus is in close conjunction with Eva's natal Neptune in the first.

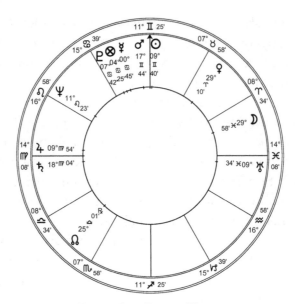

Evangeline Buys a Home
May 31, 1921 Yorktown Heights, NY 41N16 73W47
Source: Deed from Westchester County Property Records; noon chart.

Evangeline Adams tells us in her autobiography that her horoscope indicated she would be successful in her search for a new home if she could only remember that it would not come about through her own efforts. Transiting Uranus in her twelfth trined fourth house Uranus. Visiting in Westchester the next weekend, she came across an old Friends Meeting House and fell in love with it. She bought the house on May 31, 1921, with the Sun, Mars, Jupiter, Saturn and Uranus all caught up in a T-square! Transiting Saturn is approaching Eva's seventh house cusp, and an opposition to her Venus; Jupiter opposes her Jupiter. Yet Adams appears to have put greater emphasis on the heavier Uranus and its major transits to her natal chart, rather than the election itself. There were no major Solar Arcs for her at the time; progressed Mars was on her Ascendant.

Perhaps she was right. She converted the building to a lovely Colonial cottage, furnished it with her beloved American antiques, and sunk a well successfully. She seems to have enjoyed her new home in every way.

Evangeline crossed the Atlantic often, usually at least once a year, for business and pleasure. She loved to travel but usually went alone, accompanied by a secretary. We have three well-timed charts of Adams' crossings. Once again, it's difficult to say how and even if Evangeline chose them. But she could easily have selected a date and time to her liking from the many advertisements and departure schedules in the daily paper.

The first of these charts is for Evangeline's honeymoon trip on the Mauretania; this is the only journey on which her husband accompanied her. The chart is similar to the wedding election, as they left less than a week after the marriage. Dr. Broughton says,

> In beginning a journey, choose that day and hour in which the Moon and the lord of the Ascendant are in good aspect in the nativity. Let the eleventh and third houses, with their lords, be fortunate. (Broughton p. 291)

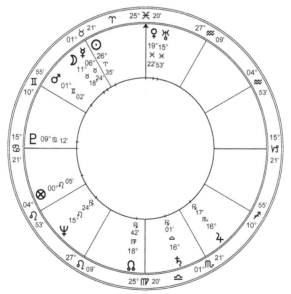

Mauretania Sailing
April 17, 1923 10:00 AM EST
New York, NY 40N43 74W00
Source: Date *from New York Herald* feature of April 7, 1923;
time from *New York Times* listings of April 16, 1923.

Here the Cancer Ascendant leads directly to the Moon in the eleventh, exalted in Taurus, conjoining Mercury and sextiling the Ascendant, Venus and Uranus in the ninth house of travel; all good for the beginning of a voyage. As is typical of Adams' elections, although the Moon will square Neptune and oppose Jupiter, its exalted placement by sign lessens the stress of these aspects. The Sun, Venus and Saturn are also exalted. The couple departed on a Thursday – a Jupiter day.

The third is ruled by the exalted Sun in Aries in the tenth house, making for a lively time, and the lord of the eleventh is Venus exalted in the ninth, providing for a pleasant and relaxing trip.

Saturn's opposition to the Sun is still in evidence, but it is a wide opposition now and out of parallel, both mitigating circum-stances. As the *New York Herald* article explained, the couple had planned on opening a branch office in England as part of the trip. They were seemingly unsuccessful in this venture, however, as it was never mentioned again.

Broughton concludes that,

> The eighth house shows what will happen to the traveler when he comes to the end of his journey and the seventh house what will happen to him on the day he returns.

Both are ruled by Saturn in the fourth: back to home and the routine of work, as usual, for Evangeline! And unfortunately, it could have also signified the end of any romantic illusions Adams may have had about her marriage.

Aside from the strength of several planets, there are some diffi-culties with the chart for Evangeline's Berengaria sailing. Although Sagittarius rises, which is nice for a long trip, Saturn is conjunct the Ascendant. (Saturn figures importantly in all three travel charts, but Adams had natal Saturn in Sagittarius in the ninth.) Saturn is, however, part of a wide grand trine involving Jupiter and Neptune.

Dr. Broughton had said that it is bad for journeys,

...to have Saturn or Mars in the third or ninth house, but much worse to have them, or either of them, in the second house.

Here, Mars is in the second, so this is the worst, in his opinion. We also have a full Moon, which promises some surprises. We've gotten used to Evangeline's usual selection of Pisces planets, but here Mercury and Venus both square Saturn between the third and first houses. This chart is certainly not ideal.

But the Sun is conjunct Jupiter, the Sun and Venus are exalted, and Jupiter is in one of the signs of its triplicity. Mercury is in its fall and has just passed the square of Saturn. With all of her Aquarius, Evangeline seems at times willing to try out and experiment with almost anything. She does mention, however, that she would "not fly until Mars passes by the affliction of Saturn, and that may keep me from flying at all while abroad."   It did. She returned via ship on April 24, before the square was exact.

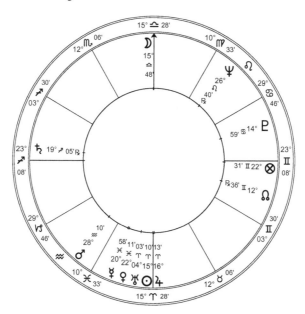

Berengaria Sailing
April 5, 1928 12:00 AM EST
New York, NY 40N43 74W00
Source: Date from E. Adams' letter of April 9, 1928;
time from *New York Times* listings of April 3, 1928.

Adams also did not have much leeway in choosing when to depart, saying in her letter of April 9 that,

> I had no idea of coming on Tuesday evening, April 3, and sailed Wednesday evening... I dictated up to within an hour before sailing, in order to get off work which had to be done before I could leave.

Transiting Uranus would exactly trine her ninth house Saturn from the first within a few weeks, attesting to her sudden departure.

As might have been expected from the chart, Eva found her room "very uncomfortable," and there was much rough and stormy weather. She noted, however, that,

> Several ships struck terrible gales all around us, so we have been most favored by Neptune. He should be good to me for I certainly love his magic power.

A significant part of this trip was astrological consulting for a group of businessmen in Berlin, which may account for the strong placement of Saturn in the chart. Adams had a wonderful time in Berlin, then returned to Paris to be fitted for some gowns, do some sightseeing, attend the opera, and dine out.

Gemini rises and the Moon sets in Sagittarius for Adams' crossing on August 22, but this is also an interesting and mixed travel election; we have another grand trine, made up this time of the Moon, Venus and Uranus. It was again an abrupt departure, as Evangeline sailed with only three days' notice, which may account for some of the less than stellar qualities of this chart. Saturn, Uranus and Pluto are in a T-square, with Mars also involved to a lesser degree. Once again, though, Saturn is in its own sign, and the planets are not parallel in declination, making the aspects less difficult than they might otherwise be. The Moon, Mercury, Ascendant T-square is less problematic, as it perfectly describes a trip, and Mercury is exalted in Virgo. As on her 1928 crossing, Evangeline had again brought her little dog, Lover, with her (she had done a horary chart to decide whether to take him along).

Adams planned to attend a four-day International Astrology Congress in Berlin the first week of September, so there was a limited selection of dates. Evangeline's health was failing, and she also visited Wiesbaden for the healing baths and thermal springs. Although pleased with the crossing, conference and treatments, there were many nagging problems on this trip. Eva found Wiesbaden to be,

> ...the oldest and most depressing place I have been in; the coffee vile, food did not seem to nourish me. I did lose flesh and I did sleep about 15 hours a day.

Although she loved Berlin:

> You get the feeling of confidence and security everywhere. No fear of being cheated or having anything stolen. What a pity our country has lost all sense of integrity.

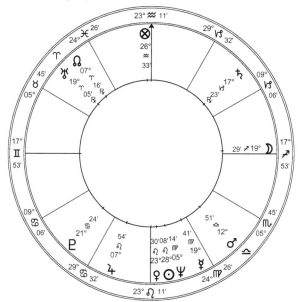

Adams Crossing
August 22, 1931 12:40 AM EDT
New York, NY 40N43 74W00
Source: Date and time from E. Adams' letter of August 22, 1931.

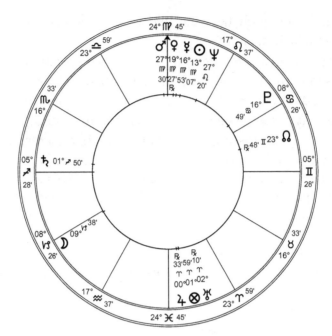

Old Glory Takes Off
September 6, 1927 12:23 PM EST
Old Orchard Beach, ME 43N31 70W23
Source: *New York Times* of September 7, 1927 and
Astrology, Your Place in the Sun, p. 320 for date and time.

Evangeline discussed the relative merits of two plane departures in her book, *Astrology, Your Place in the Sun*. She felt that the take-off time of *New York Mirror* editor Philip Payne's plane, Old Glory, was less than fortunate. This was a much-publicized attempt to cross the Atlantic, but a failed one. We can see this chart as an excellent example of one of Dr. Broughton's rules:

> Do not let Saturn be in the Ascendant, nor a fiery sign on the Ascendant, for then there will be a watery sign on the eighth house, and there will be great danger of drowning or the ship going to the bottom... (Broughton, p. 291)

The ruler of the Ascendant, Jupiter, is placed in the fourth and co-rules the fourth – an apt symbol for going right to the bottom (or even the grave!) in a big way. Mars, ruler of the twelfth, approaches an opposition. This combination is quite powerful, especially since Jupiter in the end-of-the-matter fourth conjoins Uranus and is ruled by Mars in Jupiter's detriment. Mars, of course, opposes Uranus as well. Nicholas Culpeper said,

> Consider whether the threatening planet have power to execute his will or not; for sometimes a curst cow hath short horns. (Culpeper p. 49)

Here, the horns are strong and sharp. An S.O.S. signal was received about 14 hours into the flight and then they were lost.

This chart shares a Capricorn Moon with Lindbergh's successful transatlantic flight. But in the Lindbergh chart it rules the second and is placed above the horizon (see p. 88). Here it rules the eighth and is placed below. Of course today we can see that the Moon opposes Pluto in the eighth as well. This chart is also similar to Evangeline's April 5, 1928 crossing (p. 83) – but the Moon there is above the earth and favorably disposed by Venus exalted in Pisces.

Evangeline felt that the chart for Charles Lindbergh's transatlantic flight was in "strong contrast" with the take-off of Old Glory, although the Lindbergh chart does not conform to Dr. Broughton's traditional rules for elections. Adams felt that Jupiter and Uranus in the tenth were appropriate for this event. Jupiter strong in its own sign and ruling the tenth probably led her to see this flight as successful, especially since the Moon's last aspects are a sextile to Jupiter and trines to the Sun and Mercury.

With the Ascendant just shy of two degrees, we might say the flight was a little "too soon" astrologically. However the Moon falls in the seventh house, above the horizon, so it, too, moves up and out, as does Jupiter, the most elevated planet. Contrast this with the downward motion of the Ascendant ruler and the Moon, both placed below the horizon, along with Jupiter near the IC – the lowest point – in the chart for Old Glory's flight.

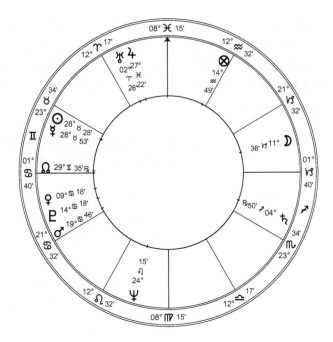

Lindbergh's Transatlantic Flight
May 20, 1927 6:51 AM LMT
Mineola, NY 40N45 73W38
Source: *Astrology, Your Place in the Sun*, p. 320.
I have translated Evangeline's "true time" to LMT.

In their book *The Day the Bubble Burst*, Gordon Thomas and Max Morgan-Witts say that Evangeline Adams,

> ...claimed correctly to have forecast Lindbergh's transatlantic flight to within 22 minutes of actual duration, foretold Rudolph Valentino's death to within a few hours; and prophesied the 1923 Tokyo earthquake to within a few days. (Thomas, p. 369)

These claims sound outrageous, and I have seen them corroborated in no other sources. Yet, the *Bubble Burst* team had scanned an incredible array of material in order to put together their book.

Could Adams have projected the length of Lindbergh's flight? Looking at the chart as a horary, the Moon in a cardinal sign and angular house suggests a time measurement in hours. And

Evangeline probably had read an estimate of the anticipated flight time.

Time Almanac 2002 lists Lindbergh's actual flight time as 33 hours, 39 minutes. If we symbolically move the Moon a degree per hour, it will conjoin the Part of Fortune in about 33 and a quarter hours, a difference of less than a half hour from the actual time.

But Evangeline would have to have known to use this direction rather than the Moon to Jupiter (ruling the tenth house of outcome) or Mercury (ruling the end-of-the-matter fourth house), both of which yield similar times of sixteen to seventeen hours!

General Forecasting

Adams' business was made up of several services. The most important were her consultations, which ordinarily lasted half an hour. For those who lived outside of New York, or could not afford a personal interview, she provided written reports. These were made up of individually typed pages describing planets in signs and houses, with some aspects included, similar to today's computerized print-outs. Adams had probably used this type of standardized report before the turn of the century and gave a delineation of natal placements, along with a forecast. Clients could also subscribe to a monthly update of their own personal charts. Her regular monthly planetary reports provided a daily guide of transit-to-transit aspects (today these are commonly seen in popular astrology magazines). The planetary report was the most in demand and included an outline of the larger cycles currently in operation. Adams' standardized report information was later incorporated into her books; descriptions of upcoming transits from Jupiter, Saturn and Uranus to the natal Sun are described in *Your Place Among the Stars*, for example.

With a Leo Moon trine Sagittarius on the Midheaven, Evangeline Adams was never one to be shy about her accom-plishments. In 1926, she told the *Pictorial Review*,

> I have seen the elder Morgan with astrology behind him, drive the
> world of finance before him. I predicted the famous Windsor fire almost
> to the hour, and escaped with my belongings from the flames. I foretold

the month in which King Edward would die, the fortnight in which Caruso would sing his last song, the day on which Charles Murphy would reach the crisis of his last illness. I prophesied Roosevelt's victories and his final defeat. I foretold the Great War, its beginning and its result.

If she tended to exaggerate, it was all in service to the popularization of astrology – and to publicize her own forecasting skills.

Adams' reputation was made primarily through forecasting, but we should bear in mind that she, like all of us, made mistakes, too. The *New York World Telegram* in its obituary of Adams reported that she had said the first Lindbergh baby would live to be "a flier like his father." He was kidnapped and murdered before he was two. And the *Telegram* on February 4, 1930 recalled that in June of 1923, Adams claimed president Warren G. Harding was "under particularly good planetary influence." He died suddenly less than two months later!

Yet Adams was shrewd enough to let the public forget her mistakes. She would repeatedly remind them only of her successes. In 1928 she smugly told the *New Yorker* magazine that, "I'm only right something more than ninety-five per cent of the time."

While she often said that it was against her principles to publicly predict the results of elections, prize fights or the daily fluctuations of the market, she occasionally did so, and had more regularly done so earlier in her career. Most often, however, she claimed to have made successful predictions for the benefit of her clients, reporting them to the public only after the fact. So at times we don't know what was actually said in advance. Yet looking at the specified charts can still be instructive. Many have been remembered because they represent correct predictions. As such, the techniques employed should be clear and the results obvious, thus helping us better understand how Evangeline actually worked.

We can get an idea of Adams' thoughts on forecasting for clients from her written reports. The following excerpt was boilerplate included with her natal mail-order readings:

It would be well to give a little thought to what constitutes life, its purpose, and to realize how each year brings its blessings and disappointments. A year of nothing but sunshine, with no rain or cloudy days, would not only become very monotonous, but all life would wither up and die. So in one's life, if a whole year passed with nothing but happy and fortunate conditions, it would get very dull and be very non-productive from a serious point of view. On the other hand, a year which brought only sorrow and misfortune, with no alleviating conditions, would be unbearable. A wise Providence has ordained that neither extreme can happen.

Every planet in the horoscope has a direct bearing on different departments in your life; during each year, favorable and unfavorable aspects among the various planets operate at the same time. For instance, Uranus, Saturn, Jupiter and Mercury may all stir the vibrations of the Sun during some part of the year. Uranus may cause one to enter a larger sphere of life; Saturn may indicate a death; Jupiter may bring an inheritance; and Mercury may cause a change or bring about a journey. Life would be too simple and uninteresting but for the variety of good and ill fortune which sooner or later falls to the lot of all. The difference between a Napoleon and a weakling is largely a matter of the experiences which life has brought to each, and the use which has been made of them. There is no royal road to wisdom. The wise man co-operates with his stars, the fool thinks he rules them, and the weak man merely accepts passively what the stars indicate or chance may bring.

In the Orient, the Wise Men of the past, who gave their lives to the study of Philosophy and the Law of Cause and Effect, made very clear that one is affected by whatever happens in proportion to the reaction through surprise induced in the individual. Even our modern alienists and others who specialize on nervous or mental diseases, often subject their patients to a surprise or shock in order to recoordinate those suffering from any of the many forms of hysteria or loss of equilibrium.

If, after reading these indications, you feel that more stress has been given to the discordant aspects, bear in mind this has been done intentionally in order that the more complete information you have regarding unhappiness, ill health, or trouble in business that may overtake you, the better able will you be to meet conditions and regulate the effect they will have upon you. Although you cannot control Fate, you can, when duly informed, largely regulate your reactions. While you may not prevent a thing from happening, or overcome the inevitable, it is yours to see that the inevitable does not overcome you.

On the other hand, if too much emphasis is not placed on a favorable aspect, when the good does come, it will be the more appreciated because it has not been too much anticipated, and comes as a surprise. Human nature tends to take too much for granted, particularly happiness. The average individual is constantly looking forward to the time when he will be happy or fortunate, instead of making the most of the blessings of the present. If, therefore, after reading these indications, your first reaction is to feel depressed, realize that nothing will ever happen to you which you will not be able either to conquer or to reap therefrom benefits in the way of valuable experience, and which will enable you to work with the tide, instead of swimming against it.

Life is made up of experiences, varying according to heredity, environment, temperament and age. The effect any event has on the life largely depends upon the disposition, the intensity of the nature, and the kind of philosophy possessed. If poised and well balanced, you will consider everything which comes to your mill as grist, and you will never be cast down, as you will realize that the wisdom you have garnered through any experience is worth the cost. The great thing, however, is to get your lesson the first time and not force Fate to repeat it again and again.

By knowing when the different aspects are due to operate, you are placed in a position where you can take greatest advantage of the good promised. Instead of swimming against the tide, you can ascertain when it is due to turn and, by waiting, allow the incoming tide to carry you along. Often, by doing exactly opposite to what you feel impelled to do, you can keep an unfriendly aspect from bringing about what is threatened, and when under harmonious vibrations, you can safely intensify your impulses and take greater risks, thereby reaping a richer harvest from whatever you may do.

If, during any particular year, the aspects threaten the death of elderly relatives, and yours have already passed on, then a death may occur in your business or social life. As another example, if scandal is indicated, and you are a very conventional and law-abiding person, then you certainly need have no fears, as nothing happens by chance. The law of cause and effect is ever working, even though it may not be apparent on the surface. There are times, however, when it is not only necessary to avoid evil, but the appearance of evil.

Dr. Smith's Reading

Dr. J. Heber Smith was Evangeline's first astrology teacher; if we examine his techniques, we might gain some insight into how she, herself, worked. Adams tells us in *Astrology, Your Place in the Sun* that,

> A remark made by the author's preceptor, Dr. J. Heber Smith, when teaching her how to erect a figure, made a deep impression. This was to the effect that the type of mind that "fussed" over the minutes and seconds in drawing up a chart never made a good astrological diagnostician, such minds being too literal and their spiritual perception too limited. As an example, he stated that the charts drawn by Professor Lister (his contemporary, and whom he considered the wisest Astrologer in his period), "looked as if a hen had walked over the paper." Dr. Smith's opinion has been borne out by the author in her own experience with pupils. Raphael, under whose supervision the ephemerides upon which all Astrologers are dependent are prepared, in drawing his charts in his daily work, does not consider it necessary to put in anything but the degrees of the planets; which still further goes to prove that the more one knows of the truths of the science, the more one realizes that he is dealing with the Cosmos and that unless the Astrologer has background, years of experience and much worldly wisdom, he is in danger of depending too much on mathematics and too little on the things that count. (*Sun* pp. 308-309)

Smith had the Sun and Mercury in the sign of Sagittarius (see page 11), which prefers the broad strokes to minutiae. With Uranus in

Pisces, he understood the archetypal, especially in astrology. Evangeline couldn't agree more: with her own emphasis on Neptune and Pisces, along with Sagittarius on the ninth house, she happily concurred with her teacher's point of view. In *The Bowl of Heaven* Adams says that,

> I have learned to allow myself only three to five minutes out of the precious half hour for making the intricate mathematical calculations necessary to determine the position of the planets in the chart. (p. 16)

It's important to bear in mind that Adams was therefore never a technician *per se*: specificity and exactitude were not her forte. She was not rigorously mathematical. While prominent astrologers at the turn of the century like Dr. Luke D. Broughton and W.H. Chaney utilized Primary Directions, these would not have been in Evangeline's toolkit. Given that her typical readings lasted only a half hour, she certainly didn't have time for involved calculations in her clients' charts. She concentrated, instead, on broad principles. Thus, for example, we find her discussing astrological cycles rather than rectification.

Adams never forgot her first astrological reading with Dr. Smith:

> The first time I went to see the great diagnostician, he asked me the date and hour and place of my birth – questions which I have since asked so many thousands of times! – and made out the horoscope chart showing the position of the stars when I was born. Then he amazed me by saying:
>
> "Didn't you break your leg when you were nine years old?" (*Bowl* p. 28)

Evangeline remembered the incident well, and confirmed that it happened as she was about to turn nine. How did Dr. Smith come up with this salient fact? He must have used rough Solar Arcs to quickly determine some significant life events. If we look at the chart for Evangeline that Smith drew up, we can see that Mars is near the Ascendant and is nine degrees from the Sun. Since Smith was a medical man, an accident (Mars) related to the leg (Aquarius) would have been what leapt to his mind.

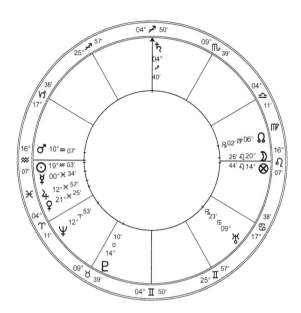

Evangeline – Earlier Time
February 8, 1868 Jersey City, NJ 40N44 74W04
Source: *The Bowl of Heaven*; time is an estimate.

Dr. Smith told me many things that seemed remarkable to me then, but which now – with my own experience of astrology's range and infallibility – are nothing more than routine. He said that I would not marry the man to whom I was then engaged. And I didn't. He said that a much richer man would propose to me during the following year. And he did. He told me that I would never have another planetary aspect in my whole life that would be apt to bring a proposal from a millionaire. And I haven't! (*Bowl* p. 311)

In remarking on Evangeline's potential marriage, Dr. Smith was using a very old technique that goes back to Ptolemy. Dr. Luke D. Broughton had reiterated it in his book, *Elements of Astrology*. Like Dr. Smith, Dr. Broughton was another homeopathic physician, as were his father and grandfather before him; they all practiced astrology as well. Broughton's father had even taught Dr. Smith's colleague Professor Lister astrology.

Broughton came to Philadelphia from Leeds in the late 1850's, and along with his brothers began publishing astrological journals beginning in the early 1860's. Dr. Smith attended Hahnemann Medical College in Philadelphia, graduating as valedictorian of his class in 1866 – the year that Dr. Broughton relocated to New York City. So their paths could easily have crossed, and it seems likely that Broughton or his brothers were an influence on Smith; Evangeline's work certainly reflects his influence as well.

Dr. Broughton put an emphasis on the regularity of planetary cycles, whose repetitions were determined by natural laws. He felt that natural laws thus governed the influence of astrology, too. Like scientists, he implied that the tenets of Christianity and astrology were not compatible. Broughton was methodical in his work, and gave definite rules for delineating the horoscope. What he was striving for was an obvious, workable method that could be successfully replicated by the student. Here is his advice on interpreting the natal potential for marriage:

> In all female horoscopes, we first see what aspect and what planet the Sun first applies to, and whether that aspect is a fortunate aspect, and that planet a fortunate planet. If the Sun first makes an evil aspect of an evil planet, say to a conjunction, square or opposition, of either Saturn or Mars, then that female, if she marries, will have an unhappy married life, especially if there are evil planets in the seventh house (the house of marriage), or evil planets aspecting the seventh house, or if the lord of the seventh house is an evil planet, and is any way afflicted by evil aspects, especially by being in square or opposition to Saturn or Mars.
>
> Those aspects in a female's nativity which the Sun makes either good or evil, to either Neptune, Uranus or the Moon are not to be noticed, as she never or hardly ever marries the person described by those planets; she will probably keep company with persons described by those planets; and if the Sun makes evil aspects to them, either conjunction, square, or opposition, the native may meet much unhappiness, if not disgrace by the persons described by those planets. (Broughton p. 164-165)

Dr. Smith was simply utilizing Dr. Broughton's rule when he analyzed Evangeline's horoscope. In the chart he drew up (p. 95), we see that the Sun's next aspect is an opposition to the Moon; the Sun-Moon opposition even straddles the Ascendant-Descendant axis, and the Sun rules the seventh house as well. So Evangeline's first engagement would not work out: she says this was correct. Smith, of course, was on extraordinarily solid astrological ground: Ptolemy, himself, had long before proposed exactly the same mode of analysis in Chapter V of his *Tetrabiblos*:

> If, however, the relative positions of the luminaries be in signs inconjunct, or in opposition, or in quartile, the cohabitation will be speedily dissolved upon slight causes, and the total separation of the parties will ensue. (Ashmand, p. 125)

Evangeline, herself, later utilized this rule. At her famous fortune-telling trial in 1914, she had justified herself by quoting published astrological authorities, and reiterated the horoscope interpretation she had given the undercover detective posing as a client:

> She gave me the date of the daughter. I told her that the Sun was unfriendly to Herschel and that that indicated that she would not marry or be likely to marry the first man to whom she was engaged, that she must be careful about her friendships, as it indicated temptations. (Coleman, p. 41).

We can see the technique clearly at work in the horoscope of Evangeline's friend, Louise Chandler Moulton. Moulton wrote many books and was the Boston correspondent on literary topics for the *New York Tribune* for many years. Her marriage to a Boston publisher at the age of twenty seems to have been fortuitous, but she remained unhappy with him. Evangeline tells us in *The Bowl of Heaven* that,

> Her husband was a fine, devoted, but extremely conservative man, with whom at times she became very much dissatisfied. (p. 42)

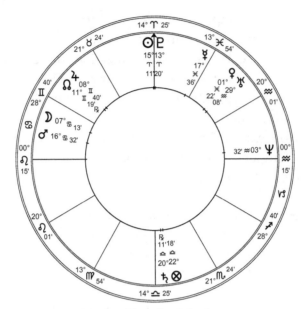

Louise Chandler Moulton
April 5, 1835 Pomfret, CT 41N54 71W58
Source: *Appleton's Cyclopaedia* Vol. IV; noon chart.

Even without a correct birth time, we can see Moulton's frustration with the man in her life. Her Aries Sun first approached a square to Mars and then an opposition to Saturn. Dr. Broughton had equated both with an "unhappy marriage." Even so, after her husband's death in 1898, Moulton confessed to Adams that now that she had her freedom, it was worthless compared with her husband's love and support.

Dr. Smith's next forecast regarding another marriage proposal for Evangeline was more easily divined. She probably visited Dr. Smith at around age nineteen, when she and her mother had moved to Boston. Transiting Uranus trined her Sun for the first time in late 1888 – perhaps this also coincided with her introduction to astrology and Dr. Smith. But in 1889, the following year, Uranus would exactly trine Adams' Sun two more times. Since the Sun rules the men in one's life in a woman's horoscope, and Dr. Smith's chart for Evangeline placed the Sun ruling the Leo seventh house, this aspect makes sense. It is also a "once in a lifetime" event, and so fits Smith's description. Since

Dr. Smith saw Uranus transiting Evangeline's eighth, it's obvious why he thought the man in question would be wealthy.

Smith also said,

> When you come before Saint Peter... I will tell him that the fact you have no children is not to be held against you. Your horoscope denies you offspring of your own. But it indicates that you are better able to rock the cradle of the world than the cradle of one child. (*Bowl* p. 31)

Perhaps he was reading Uranus in her fifth house of children, or Mercury ruling the fifth in a square aspect to Saturn. But the Sun-Moon opposition, of course, also comments on the native's children and family, since they are related to the Moon. Ellen H. Bennett, writing at about the same time as Dr. Broughton, says of this aspect that,

> Quarrels with the family occur. His parents separate, his children die or act amiss. (Bennett p. 238)

All of these things were true in Evangeline's case, however she avoided any difficulty with children by not having any. Dr. Smith's experience with medical astrology may have provided more details about her ability to conceive.

Evangeline's interview with Dr. Smith gave her many more insights:

> You are not only a born astrologer, and should take up the study of the science, but you should go a long way with it. Fear was left out of your horoscope. I doubt if you fear man, God or devil. (*Bowl* p. 33)

Evangeline's prominent Sun-Mars conjunction in Aquarius must have led to this statement, especially as Mars ruled Evangeline's ninth house.

> He told me that I had an influential planet in the house of travel, which would make me visit many foreign countries. And I have done so... In fact, he told me with startling accuracy the basic facts of my life. (*Bowl* p. 31)

Mars ruling the ninth and conjoined with the Ascendant would have also led to a conclusion of much travel. Jupiter in Pisces in the first house indicates that travel would come easily to her. But despite the specificity and supposed accuracy of Smith's reading, he was looking at the wrong chart!

> One thing bothered him. I gave him the hour of my birth as seven in the morning. But he insisted that it could not be true, as the zodiacal sign rising at that moment indicated a person of much slighter build and fairer complexion.
>
> "But, Dr. Smith," I protested, "My mother said it was seven o'clock."
>
> "She ought to know," he replied: and then added with true professional bluntness: "But if you had been born at that time, you would have been very beautiful."
>
> Apparently, that settled it. He proceeded to draw up my chart for half past eight o'clock – a time which coincided with my personal appearance. And years later, when I had almost forgotten this feature of my first astrological interview, I found an old diary of my father's in the attic of my brother's house in Chicago. In this diary, he had recorded the exact moment when each of his children came into the world. Mine was "8:30 in the morning." (*Bowl* pp. 31-32)

The ruler of Evangeline's 7:00 o'clock Ascendant was Saturn, which should make one on the slim side. Aquarius, especially with the Sun in the first house, is usually of middle to tall stature. Adams was stout, short, and plain, certainly not a description that coincides with the Sun rising. Dr. Broughton associated Aquarius with light, flaxen hair; Evangeline's was darker. Her complexion, too, was not as fine as Dr. Broughton expected from this sign. Pisces rising, he thought, should give her,

> A short stature, not very well made; a good large face, pale complexion, the body fleshy or swelling; not very straight, but stooping somewhat with the head when walking. (Broughton p. 98)

This much more accurately describes Adams as she appears in photographs. A *New Yorker* interview described her in 1928 as "very short, plump without being bulky and walks with a slight limp." The limp was the result of a riding accident in the summer of 1922. She had felt she was under "accidental conditions" with transiting Uranus on her Ascendant ruler, Jupiter, and transiting Mars in Sagittarius (relating to horses and riding) squaring it from the ninth. Although she took the precaution of riding a gentle animal, Evangeline was thrown anyway.

Adams' New Horary

Evangeline felt that her main contribution to astrological forecasting was a method which she referred to as a "new horary." Adams utilized the transiting Ascendant and houses. Then she would turn the client's natal chart, and read the turned chart. This method is quick and easy, as there is no need to erect a full horary figure. And it came in handy in cases where the client had no time of birth. As it is a simplified method, it's well to note that Adams felt it only worked for current concerns, or the immediate future. And yet, in utilizing the client's chart as an integral part of the new horary, it seems logical that the answers given will be well suited to the native's feelings about the situation at hand. This excerpt is from *The Bowl of Heaven*:

The ancients, in their horary astrology, considered only the mundane position of the heavens at the time the individual sought an answer to his query. I consider also the position of the heavens in relation to the individual's own chart. The difference may seem trivial. But every competent astrologer who reads these words will know that it is fundamental and I assert as a fact, which I have established after years of research and experimentation, that if I draw my conclusions from the position of the planets in combination with the chart of the individual at the moment I am asked to decide a given question, I will get my answer – and it will be the right answer.

This is my method. I note the degree that is rising at the moment my client enters. I then adjust his chart so the corresponding degree in the chart will be an "Accidental Ascendant," and proceed to read the horoscope as if it were the radix.

My first caller after I had finally convinced myself that I had at last found this most important of all keys to the astral vaults, was a woman who lived in Lexington, Massachusetts. I drew her radical chart as usual, placing the planets in their proper places in the circle. I then adjusted the chart as described above and I discovered that Saturn, the indicator of worry and misfortune, was, at the moment of her question, in that portion of the heavens which rules brothers and sisters. So I asked her if by any chance she was worried about her brother's health. She replied: "Why, that is just what I am here for. My brother is very ill." I asked for the dates of the brother's wife, drew up her horoscope, adjusted it and found her Saturn to be in the seventh house, governing the husband. His mother's Saturn, by the same process, fell in the fifth house, governing offspring. I remember this case with especial vividness, because it came as a culmination and an immediate practical verification of my years of scientific research. Since that time, I have had thousands of other confirmations. I have them every day – with every client.

Just as the position of Saturn indicates the source of worry, so all the planets tell their story and show on the adjusted astrological clock the joys, successes and possible misfortunes that may befall the questioning client in the immediate future. Whenever the ever-changing Moon appears in this so-called "Accidental Ascendant," I feel sure a journey or change is contemplated or that the opportunity for travel will soon be presented. If Mars, the planet which governs the warrior and the surgeon, and also accidents and quarrels, is the first to rise, I then feel sure that an operation, an accident or a quarrel will be the first happening to engage my caller.

If I find the planet Neptune holds the ascendancy, I feel positive that some form of intrigue or camouflage is just ahead. In some cases, instead of the deception coming from the outside world, it means that the individual is self-deceived and must not take his own ideas too seriously, or try to put through the scheme which he may have in mind at that moment. If the intuitive planet Uranus by any chance is about to rise, I then tell my client that he must not take too seriously any seemingly promised good or threatened misfortune, as it will be the unexpected that will actually happen. If Venus, the Sun or Jupiter chance to bestow their beneficent influence by being the first to rise, I know that a new love, a new honor, or a new blessing is imminent; and, regardless of the position of other planets in the chart, indicating either ill or good fortune, I know that my consultant's own life and happiness is assured for the moment, and that his immediate future will be rosy.

Let me give an illustration of this "new horary." About a year ago an old client, a Tammany leader, entered my studio at a time when in his adjusted chart Uranus was about to rise. Without waiting for him to say anything, I warned him against going into any venture at that time as it would not be practical.

Because of his established confidence in the science he shelved the contemplated project without further discussion. About a month ago he insisted on giving me the details, and at this time Saturn was rising. I told him that the indications were even less promising than before. Either the scheme would die or someone essential to it would die. Again he accepted my decision and did not invest.

I have just left the telephone. He tells me that I am right again. "Last night J.J. Frawley dropped dead at Dixville Notch." This gentleman, at one time State Senator and prominent leader in the great organization of Tammany Hall, was the one essential to the project. (*Bowl* p. 18-22)

The destruction of the Windsor Hotel by fire on March 17, 1899 was one of the defining moments of Evangeline Adams' early career (transiting Saturn conjoined her Midheaven at the time). She had come to visit New York City shortly before. After being forbidden from practicing astrology at the posh Fifth Avenue Hotel, she and her secretary registered at the very up-scale Windsor. While Adams claimed that her prediction of the fire the day before it occurred was reported to the press by proprietor Warren Leland, only her own comments can be found, and these after the fact. The following is from the *New York World* on March 20, 1899:

> Mr. Leland had asked me to read his palm. I saw that there was evil in store for him somewhere according to his horoscope and told him so. I told him that I foresaw evil not only for him but for all New York. In fact, I believed that the next day would be marked by some dire calamity. I told him that the lines in his hand indicated he had but three children. He had four I knew. We both laughed at this, but it was evident that he was worried.

Leland's wife and favorite daughter were killed in the fire and the *New York Evening Journal* on March 18 reported him to be weak, suffering and completely broken-down. He died shortly thereafter. Regardless of what Evangeline actually told her client, it would be instructive to know what she saw in his chart, as the timing of the event must have been astrological.

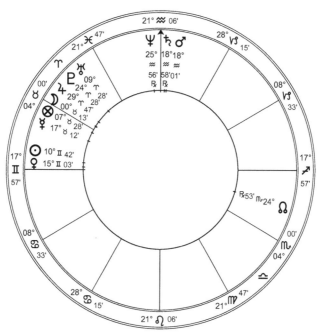

Warren F. Leland
June 1, 1845 4:55 AM LMT
Londonderry, VT 43N12 72W29
Source: *A Thousand and One Notable Nativities* cites a 1908-1909 issue of
Coming Events; data extrapolated from placements,
with place from the *NY Evening Journal* of April 5, 1899.

With Cancer on the second house, ruled by an exalted Moon in Taurus conjunct Jupiter, Warren F. Leland, the proprietor of the famous Windsor Hotel, was wealthy and earned his living by providing food and shelter on a grand scale. These and his twelfth house planets attest to the Windsor's reputation as a calm, domestic and comfortable place, where many invalids registered for long- term stays. One of Leland's favorite pursuits was relaxing by the hotel's flower garden. (See Noel Tyl's *Prediction in Astrology*, p. 30, for his fascinating rectification of Leland's chart.) Evangeline's involvement with Leland in this important crisis can easily be seen in her Sun's conjunction with his Mars, Saturn and Midheaven.

There were several indications that could point to important life developments for Leland at the time. Progressed Mercury, his ruler, and progressed Venus, the planet natally conjunct his Ascendant, were both in exact conjunction with the IC. This could imply he was approaching a new phase in life, or even nearing the fourth house "end of the matter." Solar Arc Mars was conjunct natal Uranus, signifying the possibility of a sudden and perhaps even violent event.

Transiting Uranus at 8° Sagittarius was retrograding away from an opposition to Leland's Sun, having just made a station. Saturn was transiting his seventh house and sextiling the MC and Neptune. Neptune was conjunct Leland's Ascendant and trine his MC, but past exactitude and moving slowly direct from a station earlier in the month (some accounts mention the fact that Leland had been recuperating from an illness). Transiting Pluto, not yet discovered at the time of the reading, was nearly 14° Gemini, conjunct both Leland's Sun and Venus. While all of these influences combine to make for quite a significant period of time, in none of them do we see any specific indication of what could produce such an immediate calamity the following day.

Evangeline probably utilized her "new horary" technique to answer her client's questions regarding the immediate future. In *The Bowl of Heaven*, she tells us that the reading for Warren Leland was done at about eight o'clock in the evening (p. 37). She would take the Ascendant at the time of the question, in this case about 20° Libra, turn the client's chart so that 20° Libra ascended, and read the new natal placements. Leland's natal Sun and Mercury fell in the eighth house, which could indicate heavy emotional situations and perhaps death, destruction or financial losses. Leland's Mars and Saturn fell in the turned fourth house, which rules the home (the hotel was his residence) as well as the end of life. These placements could indicate difficulties not only for Leland, but his family as well. Leland's Moon and Jupiter do fall in the seventh, promising publicity or important relationship issues, but we now know that Pluto was conjunct the Descendant as well.

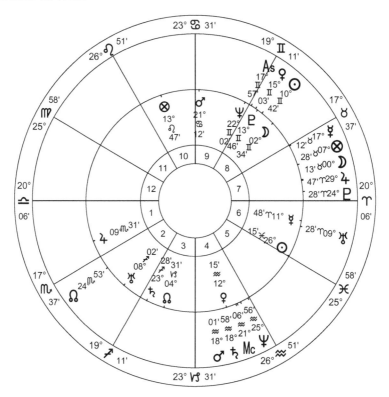

Leland Reading
March 16, 1899 8:00 PM EST
New York, NY 40N43 74W00
Inner Chart: Evangeline's reading Outer: Leland
Source: *The Bowl of Heaven* for the time; newspaper accounts for date.

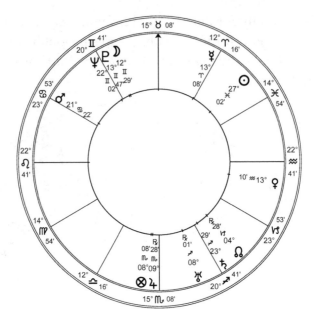

The Windsor Hotel Fire
March 17, 1899 3:10 PM EST
New York, NY 40N43 74W00
Source: *The World, New York,* March 18, 1899.

Leland died on April 4, 1899 from appendicitis. The appendix was successfully removed on April 1, but his distraught emotional condition created complications.

The exact time of the fire was 3:10 p.m. It burned extremely quickly, with all of the hotel's walls down by 4:30. The Moon and Pluto in the tenth house opposite Uranus in the fire chart point toward a sudden and violent event. The transiting T-square of Sun, Saturn and Neptune is given an immediate outlet through Saturn's trine and Neptune's sextile to the Ascendant. Mars had no hard major aspects, but it was out of bounds in declination (24N50) and paralleled the out of bounds Moon at 24N12. It's also interesting to note that the hotel itself was probably experiencing a Saturn return, as it was nearly thirty years old when it burned to the ground.

But this was a lucky day for Evangeline, as she would leave unharmed and get much publicity as a result of the fire. The transit Sun conjoined her Ascendant, and her progressed Sun and Jupiter were approaching a conjunction with her natal Venus and Ascendant. The transiting Saturn-Neptune opposition approached her fourth-tenth house axis, while still trining and sextiling her natal Moon. And transiting Jupiter in Scorpio was in partile trine to her natal Uranus, and forming a grand trine with natal Jupiter. Transiting Jupiter did square Adams' Mars as well, but this was, indeed, a frightening situation.

In *Astrology, Your Place in the Sun*, Evangeline tells us of the tragic fate of Philip Payne, Managing Editor of the *New York Daily Mirror*, as he attempted to fly to Rome from the U.S.:

> He was for some years a client of the author, and, at the time his chart was consulted as to whether this feat would meet with success, his Saturn, Uranus, and Mars were all about to rise, clearly indicting the long delays before starting off, the unexpected happenings, and the ultimate disaster which overtook him and his companions. (*Sun* p. 319-320)

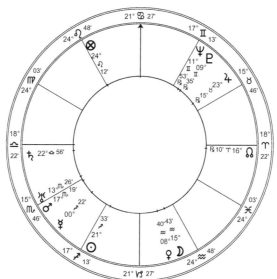

Philip A. Payne
December 13, 1893 New York, NY 40N43 74W00
Source: Date from *Who Was Who in Journalism 1925-1928*;
time reflects Adams turning the chart at the consultation.

Previous transatlantic flights had only been made to France and Germany at the time, so the venture was risky. Payne's flight was sponsored by William Randolph Hearst, and was delayed from its scheduled take-off for a few days as they awaited government approval of the plane and the arrival of fuel. The editor traveled with two pilots, all of whom lost their lives. After take-off, the plane was sighted east of Newfoundland, but an S.O.S. was received a few hours later, and the plane was declared lost on September 8, with the wreckage being found the following week. Experts speculated on what had gone wrong – a storm, engine overloading or motor problems – but in the end no one really knew what happened.

Since we have no time for Payne's birth, I've turned his chart to appear as Evangeline described. The time of Payne's consultation with Adams placed his Saturn, Uranus and Mars rising, an ominous indication (Evangeline did tend to generalize about what was "rising"; for her, it could point to the whole eastern side of the chart!) And if she had advised her regular client to avoid this risky venture, why did he take the trip anyway?

Natal Readings

In his biography, Sidney Kirkpatrick quoted the astrological reading Edgar Cayce did for himself in 1919 while in a trance state:

> ...Uranus [is] at its zenith, hence the body is 'ultra' in its actions... Hence [there is] no middle ground for this body: [he is] very good or very bad, very religious or very wicked, very rich or always losing, very much in love or hate, very much given to good works or always doing wrong... As to the forces of this body [Edgar Cayce] the 'psychical' is obtained through action of Uranus and of Neptune always it has been to this body and always will... This body will either be very rich or very poor.

Over four years later, Cayce traveled to New York City and had his horoscope read by Evangeline Adams. Kirkpatrick says,

Edgar reported being quite impressed by the horoscope she gave him, for it was similar to that of the previous reading he had given on himself. And as Edgar later reported, much of what she said would later "prove to be true." There was only one thing about the horoscope that he found disturbing. "Resign yourself never to achieve [complete] success or to be [materially] happy." (Kirkpatrick, p. 272; bracketed notes are Kirkpatrick's)

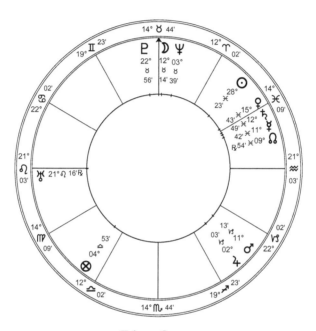

Edgar Cayce
March 18, 1877 3:03 PM LMT
Hopkinsville, KY 36N52 87W29
Source: *Edgar Cayce: An American Prophet.*

Mercury, ruler of the second house, placed in its detriment and closely conjunct Saturn, relates to Cayce's finances, which were always precarious. Mercury also conjoins the eighth house cusp, further signifying finances. One might imagine the Moon in Taurus conjunct the Midheaven to point toward success in the career, especially since it trines Mars in Capricorn. But perhaps Venus, ruling the tenth house of career, also conjoining Saturn in the eighth house, led Adams to her negative conclusion as well.

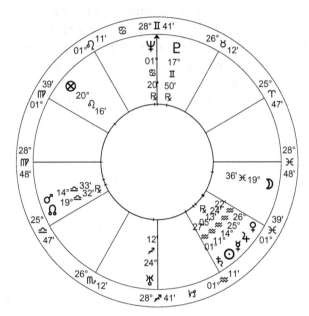

Tallulah Bankhead
January 31, 1903 9:00 PM CST
Huntsville, AL 34N44 86W35
Source: *Astrodatabank* gives this data a "DD" rating due to conflicting reports.
It quotes Jensen in *World Astrology* from July 1951, citing Bankhead –
so this is the chart Adams would have used.

Actress Tallulah Bankhead had made her stage debut in New York City in 1919, she but hadn't had much success before she consulted Evangeline Adams in the summer of 1922. Adams stated in *The Bowl of Heaven* that she told Tallulah "you are under particularly good conditions right now for traveling and for success abroad." (*Bowl* p. 84) Tallulah concurred:

> Miss Adams told me my future lay across the water. I was about to be paged from afar. In dismissing me she said, "Go if you have to swim." (Bankhead, p. 91)

Evangeline was clearly looking at transits to the natal chart, one of the most common astrological techniques for forecasting. Jupiter rules long-distance travel, and Jupiter in Libra that fall would give

Bankhead success through travel as it sextiled Uranus and created a grand trine with her Jupiter, Venus and Midheaven.

Tallulah would not have such a good combination with Jupiter for another 12 years! Jupiter would go on to trine her Moon in early '23, further insuring success. Tallulah also had favorable transits from Saturn, which point toward career efforts that can generate a lasting success. Saturn in the first house in Libra would be trining the actress' Sun and Mercury during late 1922 and parts of 1923, making for an excellent time to develop her career.

Jupiter came through in the form of luck, a foreign gentleman, and an opportunity abroad. Bankhead met the British producer Charles Cochran in New York in the fall of 1922. He returned to England and cabled her about an engagement with the famous manager Sir Gerald du Maurier. Yet Cochran soon cabled that the engagement was off; another actress had already been engaged. But with the stick-to-it-iveness of five planets in fixed signs, and the confidence Adams inspired, Bankhead borrowed money and made the trip anyway. When du Maurier met her, he agreed Tallulah must have the part. Bankhead's role in *The Dancers* in 1923 launched her career and began eight years of stage success in London.

In *The Bowl of Heaven*, Adams congratulated herself on her correct forecast for Theodore Roosevelt, Jr. (p. 132). Always admiring of Aquarians and ever-attracted to celebrity, she was likely to have been much interested in the President's daughter, Alice, who was an Aquarian like herself and a media darling given to flout convention. The birth of her daughter, Paulina, also garnered much attention, and the little girl was immediately dubbed "The Valentine's Baby." Evangeline included a thumbnail sketch of the baby's horoscope in her autobiography:

The first thing I noticed was that Neptune was in her house of birth, at the moment she was born, which meant that the child was not destined to stay where she was born. And she didn't. The moment her mother was able to leave the hospital in Chicago, she and Paulina caught a train for Washington, D.C. The baby also had Jupiter, the planet ruling money, in good aspect to Saturn, ruling older people, and Uranus, ruling the unusual. This combination indicated that she would profit through older persons – and in unusual ways. The next newspaper bulletin concerning Paulina Longworth told of a bequest of five thousand dollars as a savings bank nest egg from one of her mother's wealthy friends in Chicago. And, a few weeks later, I read somewhere that her mother had received a similar sum from a manufacturer of a well-known face cream for a written testimonial – and that Mrs. Longworth explained this unusual action on the ground that she was giving the money to her daughter Paulina.

There are other indications in this baby's horoscope – as there are in every baby's – that the parents should be glad to consider in mapping her future life. Paulina has Venus in Aquarius, a human sign in aspect to a practical planet, Mars. This combination has produced some of the world's greatest artists. She also has Mercury in Aquarius, indicating possibilities as a writer or inventor. Both of these aspects are especially desirable in this, the Aquarian or humanitarian age. And she has Jupiter in her house of travel, indicating that she will very likely spend much time in foreign lands, and that she will prosper away from home. This is a sign that is hard to beat. And the wise parent who knows about it won't try. Cecil Rhodes had this sign; and in spite of his great abilities, he never made good at home. What he did when he went to South Africa all the world knows. So I say to Alice Longworth, as a piece of unsolicited advice: If Paulina wishes to travel, let her go. (*Bowl*, pp. 174-175)

This breezy, upbeat forecast seems to imply a rosy future. And true to Evangeline's interpretation for the baby, she grew up to love literature, languages and poetry. (Adams associated Venus square Mars with "artists" like J.M.W. Turner, Goethe, W.B. Yeats and George Sand, whose charts she presented in *Astrology, Your Place Among the Stars*.)

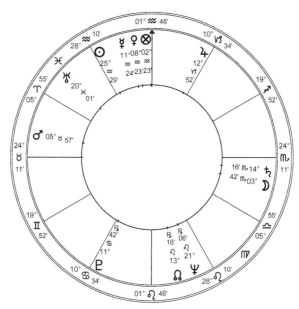

Paulina Longworth
February 14, 1925 10:30 AM CST
Chicago, IL 41N52 87W39
Source: *Princess Alice* by James Brough, p. 268.

Evangeline clearly had a timed chart (the birth data would have appeared in the papers since the baby's mother was famous) and must have chosen to ignore some of the more difficult configurations in the horoscope. The Sun is in detriment in Aquarius and opposes Neptune. Paulina idolized her father, a popular long-term Congressman and Speaker of the House, who was also a heavy drinker and philanderer who died when she was only eight. (Alice's "unusual action" of endorsing products was due to the fact that her husband always lived beyond his means.) Paulina never seemed to recover from the loss of her father; on the eve of her marriage at age nineteen, her mother told her that her biological father was really a Washington Senator. Since the Sun rules the men in one's life, it's no surprise that Paulina's husband was also a drinker who died of cirrhosis of the liver when she was just 27.

With Mercury and Venus in the tenth house one would expect some prominence. Traditionally, the tenth house rules the mother and aptly describes Paulina's witty, sociable and charming Aquarian mom. Yet Evangeline neglected to mention that these two planets were part of a wide T-square also involving the Moon, Mars and Saturn. With the Moon in its detriment in Scorpio opposing Mars in its detriment in Taurus and conjoining Saturn, Paulina's relationship with her mother was difficult. She was never able to live up to what the more charismatic woman expected of her.

Despite the attractive face and figure promised by Taurus rising, Paulina was described as immensely shy, unkempt, sullen and awkward, with a pronounced stutter and a crippling lack of self-confidence. She suffered from Saturn, ruler of three houses and four planets at the top of her chart. The violent and dangerous fixed star Algol at about 25° Taurus conjoined her Ascendant, and Mars in its detriment in the twelfth likewise made her self-destructive. Since Mars rules the seventh, her husband was obviously part of the problem. She drank heavily after her marriage and had prescriptions for sleeping pills and tranquilizers. A nervous breakdown and shock treatments followed her husband's death.

Yet despite her many woes, Longworth found some comfort in her later years. Evangeline had correctly alluded to Paulina's humanitarian impulses and accurately identified Jupiter in the ninth as a favorable indication. Paulina had done some traveling, yet with Jupiter in its fall in Capricorn, its real rewards came closer to home, such as in her enjoyment of horseback riding. Longworth later converted to Catholicism, a Capricorn religion if ever there was one due to its long and remarkably consistent tradition. She became an active hospital and homeless shelter volunteer, as befits her prominent Neptune and her service-oriented sixth house placements.

Paulina died from an overdose of a barbiturate, a tranquilizer and alcohol at age 32. (Moon conjunct Saturn in Scorpio seems an apt description of a depressive condition.) Perhaps Adams was right, after all, in pointing out only the best in the horoscope of a then one-year-old girl. Evangeline's strong Pisces influence made her sensitive and compassionate, but she also tended to want to make everyone feel good. She had said of a similarly afflicted horoscope:

The Moon was afflicted – a condition indicating trouble with her mother... Venus was afflicted – indicating danger from gossip... Jupiter was afflicted – indicating loss of fortune... I don't like to read horoscopes like that. They tend to depress me and make me less fit to help those who have more of a chance with fate. But I handle them as frankly and tactfully as I can. No one ever leaves my doors depressed or discouraged, if I can prevent it. Nor ever shall. For inspiration to others is, in my philosophy, the soul of astrology. (*Bowl* p. 116-117)

Isadora Duncan and her sister Elizabeth had been teaching a dancing class in the Windsor Hotel the day of the fateful fire. The dancer later rented a studio in Carnegie Hall, Evangeline's building, though the two don't appear to have been friends.

In 1924 or '25, as Adams prepared the manuscript for *The Bowl of Heaven*, she received a client who tried to test her skills:

Just the other day, a visitor, intent on tricking me, gave me the birth dates of two children. I went through the usual process of consulting reference books and scribbling calculations. Then I put away the charts.

"There's no use my reading these horoscopes," I said.

"Why not?" asked the visitor.

"Because both of these children are dead – dead by drowning."

The caller had given me the dates of the two children of Isadora Duncan who lost their lives when the dancer's automobile catapulted into a... river.

I was "mad" clear through, not because of the chance he had given me to rout one of astrology's enemies – I loved that! — but to think that there were still people in the world whose minds were closed to the marvelous powers of the stars. (*Bowl* p. 183)

The inference, of course, is that Adams knew from the horoscopes that the children had drowned. Yet it's unlikely her client would have even had their times of birth! Isadora's children, Deirdre and Patrick, had died on April 19, 1913 in Neuilly, France. Their nurse was taking them home, the car stalled, and the driver went out to crank the engine. Suddenly the car careened across the road and into the Seine, killing all three passengers. The well-researched biography, *Isadora: A*

Sensational Life, only includes an approximate birth time for her daughter Deirdre; her son Patrick's time is unknown to us.

Deirdre's timed chart has the North Node conjunct the Midheaven and the Sun (there was a total solar eclipse just a few days before), and hence the South Node conjoins the IC, considered the house of endings.

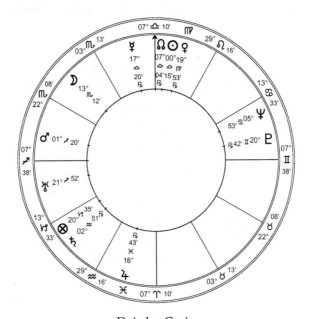

Deirdre Craig
September 24, 1903 12:00 PM GMT
Noordwijk, Netherlands 52N14 4E26
Source: *Isadora: A Sensational Life* quotes a friend's diary,
citing "around noon," page 197.

There is also a grand cross involving first house Uranus, Venus, Jupiter and Pluto (though the last hadn't yet been discovered). Certainly, the chart has some difficulties, and the afflicted Jupiter in Pisces in the third house might suggest danger near the water.

Patrick's probable Moon conjunct Uranus, with both squaring Saturn, is also a tough combination. His Venus in Pisces squares Mars conjunct Pluto, also a difficult square, but Adams would once again not have seen Pluto! (Patrick was also born near a total solar eclipse that occurred about a week after his birth.) But with or without timed charts, Adams' half-hour consultation sessions certainly didn't allow enough time to do all the necessary analyses and involved computations necessary to determine if the children could potentially die young (see Robert Zoller's *Tools and Techniques of the Medieval Astrologers* for rules for determining length of life).

Adams often studied the horoscopes of newsmakers, so was probably familiar with these charts and wanted to prove something to her skeptical client.

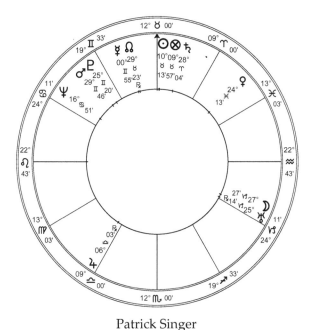

Patrick Singer
May 1, 1910 Beaulieu, France 47N07 1E01
Source: *Isadora: A Sensational Life* for the date, p. 263; noon chart.

Adams also advised the famous playwright Eugene O'Neill on business. In March of 1927, O'Neill and his wife Agnes had moved to Bermuda. According to Louis Sheaffer's biography of O'Neill, when Mrs. O'Neill was in New York City on other business,

> Agnes also, at Eugene's request, called on Evangeline Adams, the astrologist, whom Bobby [Broadway designer Robert Edmond] Jones had recommended as remarkably prescient. Miss Adams, predicting a "bad financial slump for next year for the U.S." advised the playwright "to liquidate & get all overhead expenses cut down," but she also forecast that his economic situation would "pick up about October." Her final word was that he should "close" with the Theater Guild as soon as possible. (p. 251)

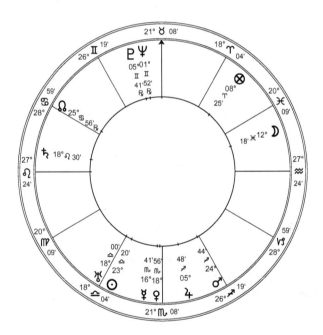

Eugene O'Neill
October 16, 1888 1:30 AM EST
New York, NY 40N43 74W00
Source: *Astrodatabank* cites Drew for the time,
but labels this "D" data, due to conflicting reports.

This little excerpt shows Adams reiterating a financial forecast for the U.S. that she'd already given to the media a number of times; in the following year, 1928, it was to prove incorrect. We can also begin to see her chain of referrals, as Robert Edmond Jones had worked for many years with the Broadway producer, Arthur Hopkins, who was also an Adams client. Jones also recommended Evangeline to O'Neill. This account is likely to be accurately recorded, as Agnes wrote her husband shortly after the reading.

The reading took place in April, 1927. O'Neill had transiting Saturn retrograding back to conjoin Jupiter in May, stationing in August, and conjoining Saturn again in October. In her posthumous book, *The Evangeline Adams Guide for 1933*, Adams says of this aspect,

> This is a temporary aspect which may make you less optimistic and which may seem to cut you off from your best fortune. This will NOT be a favorable time for making investments, or for taking any chances where money is involved. Either your expenses may be heavier, or your income may be less, but in any case, try to "cut your garment to your cloth" rather than attempt to force Fate…
>
> If you have been planning an expansion of your business, this would be a most unfavorable time to begin. You will do much better to wait until this temporary and unfavorable aspect has passed. (*1933* p. 299)

Thus her advice to "liquidate and get all overhead expenses cut down." It seems as if O'Neill took Evangeline's advice seriously. The Theater Guild had been considering productions of O'Neill's plays *Marco Millions* and *Strange Interlude*, but would not make a commitment to *Strange Interlude* until they saw a cut script. It is fascinating that the producer was pressing O'Neill to cut his typically over-written script at this time, also no doubt, due to the restrictive nature of Saturn! O'Neill subsequently pushed for the producers to accept his work and visited New York himself in mid-May, when the Guild placed both plays under option.

Adams' suggestion to wrap up his contract negotiations with the Theater Guild "asap" could relate to transiting Jupiter in the eighth trine Mercury and Venus in the third house by early April. Uranus through the eighth would also sextile tenth house Neptune exactly in May, perhaps another contractual window of oppor-tunity. Adams thought O'Neill's financial prospects should improve around October. By the end of the month, Saturn would be past its conjunction with natal Jupiter.

The well-known mythologist, writer and lecturer Joseph Campbell first visited Evangeline Adams at the age of 21, according to *A Fire in the Mind* by Stephen and Robin Larsen. The date was November 10, 1925: transiting Saturn was in square to Campbell's Saturn, and Jupiter in Capricorn was squaring his Ascendant-Descendant axis.

Adams said Campbell would make a good actor, journalist or playwright, and had a mystical bent:

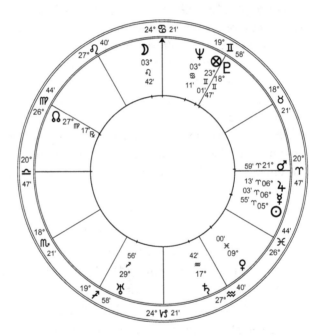

Joseph Campbell
March 26, 1904 7:25 PM EST
New York, NY 40N43 74W00
Source: *Astrodatabank* rates this "A" data, citing Campbell's mother.

She told me that I am inclined toward mysticism – that I could have been a priest, but that I would have been uncomfortable under orthodox restrictions. (Larsen p. 68)

Perhaps this related to his Ascendant ruler, Venus, placed in its exaltation in the fifth house and trining Neptune in the ninth. As Campbell had been casting about in search of his life's work, Adams advised him not to worry, that by 1927 things should begin to fall into place (Saturn would then trine his tenth house Moon). 1934, she said, should begin a period in which he would find himself consolidating his impulses and finding his own path. It was then that he was offered a faculty position at Sarah Lawrence College, where he would remain for forty years. He experienced his Saturn return in January of 1934.

As in Tallulah's forecast, we can once again see how the effects of transiting Saturn indicate important career decisions, which may concentrate the energies in a particular direction and indicate periods of stability.

While Campbell was for a time interested in astrology, he later gave it up: he didn't want to know about the future in advance. Adams had advised him against marriage with a girlfriend, but Campbell said of his wife, Jean, that,

> I found I couldn't get out of that [relationship]. Her Mars was on my Venus, and my Venus on her Mars; her Sun on my Moon and her Moon on my Sun.

Charles Lindbergh had been the country's most prized possession since his transatlantic flight in 1927. When he and his wife Anne had a baby boy, the press leapt to the scene. Frustrated by reporters, the Lindberghs revealed very little about their firstborn, but around two weeks after his birth they were forced to release a photograph when there was speculation that the baby was horribly deformed. The press had dubbed the child the "Little Eaglet," and the *New York World-Telegram* on November 11, 1932 said that Evangeline had forecast that the baby would become "a flier like his father."

Adams must have been reading the boy's Sun conjunct Jupiter in the ninth house and Mercury sextile Uranus for indications of air travel. The baby's exalted Moon and dignified Saturn formed a grand trine along with Neptune in earth signs. But there was also a wide T-square made up of the Ascendant, Saturn and Uranus. Evangeline couldn't see that Pluto created a grand cross or that the Sun-Pluto midpoint exactly opposed Saturn. The baby's Pluto is closely conjunct his Midheaven; this planet's discovery was announced just a few months before his birth and his short life was extraordinarily Plutonian. He was kidnapped on March 1, 1932 and found dead on May 12.

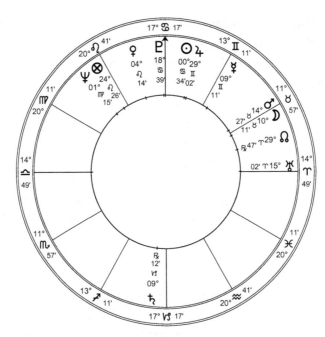

Charles A. Lindbergh III
June 22, 1930 2:10 PM EDT
Englewood, NJ 40N54 73W58
Source: Lois Rodden's *Astrodatabank* rates this "A" data, citing several sources.

Saturn, Uranus and Pluto so close to the angles presage difficulty. The Moon rules the Midheaven and translates Saturn to Mars in its detriment on the cusp of the eighth house.

It's been rumored that Evangeline's forecast of the death of Charles Lindbergh III was responsible for the "blackout" of astrology on the airwaves in subsequent years. This could not be true, as she was off the air by July of 1931, well before the boy's kidnapping. The only documented forecast I've found is the rosy one mentioned on page 124. And Evangeline, as we saw with Paulina Longworth's chart, mainly focused on the positive.

Like most astrologers, Evangeline Adams had a lot of clients who were interested in seeing what would come of their romantic relationships. For many, she had standard advice:

> My usual method, when I find a girl and a man rushing to their doom, is to suggest delay. If I ask either of them to take my word that the attraction is temporary and physical, they invariably feel that what I say might be true of the average couple, but that they are exceptions and that nothing could make them less interested in each other. But in many cases, they have the faith in the science to say: "Oh well, if by waiting a while we are going to be much happier, we'll be on the safe side and do so." They often come back to me, after waiting beyond the limit of the first physical attraction, and tell me they found that they were so completely out of harmony that they broke the engagement. (*Woman's Home Companion*, June 1925, p. 12)

Sara began working for Adams in 1919. She was still in her employ several years later when she asked Miss Adams to delineate her compatibility with her fiancé, Mark. Adams cautioned her not to marry him. Although no birth times were available, it's clear this would be a difficult relationship. Sara's Moon, Venus, Mars, Jupiter, Uranus T-square pointed toward relationship difficulties, but now we know they also formed a grand cross with Pluto. Mark's Sun, Mars and Uranus created a similar pattern, which aggravated Sara's own. Mark's family also disapproved of the match.

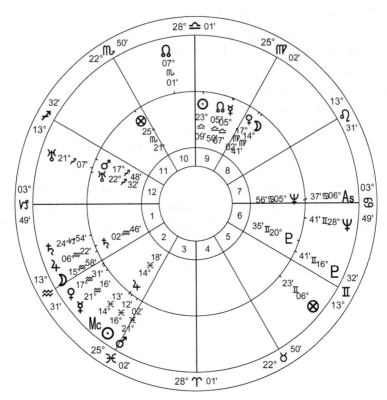

Sara (Inner wheel) October 17, 1903
Mark (Outer wheel) March 7, 1902
New York, NY 40N43 74W00
Source: Dates recorded by the family; noon charts.

The couple chose to marry anyway, as rebellious Uranian types are wont to do. Religious differences created a continual source of tension for Sara. Her Saturn conjoined her husband's Jupiter; and her Jupiter, though conjunct his Sun and Mars, squared his Uranus and Pluto. These Jupiter aspects show their different beliefs and cultural backgrounds. His Saturn also squared her Sun. She soon needed psychiatric care and was eventually institutionalized. It was only a few years after her marriage that she was released and committed suicide.

Decumbitures and Death

Evangeline's first astrology teacher, Dr. J. Heber Smith, had utilized astrology in his medical diagnoses. Adams' apprenticeship consisted of erecting horoscopes for Smith's patients, and she talked about the importance of medical elections in her autobiography.

Because of her medical astrology background and her many references to clients' health and deaths, it seems obvious that Adams had techniques that helped her analyze these affairs. Dr. Luke D. Broughton, another homeopath, included some of Cardan's and Culpeper's aphorisms on decumbitures in his comprehensive text, *Elements of Astrology*, which would have been available to Adams; Adams' teacher, Catherine Thompson, had studied directly with Dr. Broughton. So we may conclude that Evangeline had familiarity with decumbiture charts and that she utilized them in her own practice. Decumbitures are inception charts for the time an illness strikes or makes one lie down or fall ill. The most common type is read like a horary, with the patient represented by the first house, the illness by the sixth and the doctor by the seventh.

An early client of Adams' was actor Joseph Jefferson, famed for his portrayal of Rip van Winkle. Adams said that,

> It was my sad duty to foresee the great man's death, and to know in advance that it would happen within 30 days of the time it actually took place. (*Bowl*, p. 45)

This sounds like a fantastic claim, but let's see how Evangeline might have made it astrologically. Joseph Jefferson was an actor who had been a client of Adams' while she practiced in Boston from 1899 to 1905. He was a popular comedian and had made a name in such well-known shows as *Our American Cousin*, *Evangeline*, and adaptations from Dickens. He was best known, however, for his adaptation and performance of Washington Irving's *Rip van Winkle*, in which he toured extensively. A Pisces, the actor had other talents, and was also a skilled painter and expert fisherman.

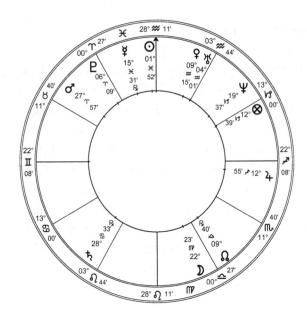

Joseph Jefferson
February 20, 1829 Philadelphia, PA 39N57 75W10
Source: *New York Times* obituary, April 24, 1905; noon chart.

Jefferson had fallen ill shortly after a visit to former President Cleveland. Although the family physician had initially diagnosed only a mild type of pneumonia, the doctor reported that the condition of the actor had become more serious on April 13, 1905 "at about noon." A front-page article in the *New York Times* considered Jefferson at this point to be "dangerously ill."

At first glance the decumbiture does not look that difficult. The exalted Sun in Aries rules the Ascendant and is high in the sky, signifying strength and vitality. The benefics Venus and Jupiter are in the tenth house with Venus ruling the Midheaven in its own sign. If we stopped here, we might say that Jefferson would recover. But the Sun has no close major aspects except its application by sextile to Saturn, ruler of the sixth house of disease, indicating that the illness progresses. Saturn's position on the cusp of the eighth is a classic indication of an illness ending in death, confirming the physician's eventual diagnosis that this was a serious condition.

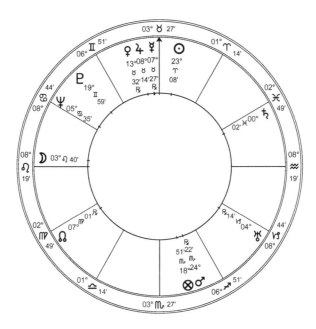

Jefferson's Condition Worsens
April 13, 1905 12:00 PM CST
Palm Beach, FL 26N42 80W02
Source: *New York Times*, April 14, 1905.

The Moon conjunct the Ascendant is a questionable placement that indicates a changeable condition, especially since it is actually placed in the twelfth house and rules the twelfth. Its placement in Leo may be thought to produce more vitality, but in decumbiture, the Moon in fixed signs suggests a stubborn illness. The Moon squares Mercury and Jupiter, the most elevated planets, showing difficulty in expressing physical vitality. Also problematic is the fact that Jupiter is ruler of the eighth: placed in the tenth it dominates the chart, squaring not only the Moon but exactly squaring the Ascendant as well.

While none of these conditions are completely conclusive, they have a cumulative effect. And Saturn on the cusp of the eighth makes death a very real possibility. Saturn also rules the seventh house and is placed in Pisces, clearly a most appropriate significator of the physician who had initially diagnosed the condition as only mild. With Saturn also squaring Mars in Scorpio in the fourth house, we could say that the doctor sent his patient directly to the grave! Saturn in Pisces can indicate pneumonia and Saturn also rules the sixth house, which describes the illness.

Yet how could Adams have forecast death within thirty days of April 23, the date of the actual death, as she claimed? She would have had the information from the *Times*, and she presumably had Jefferson's full birth chart from consultations, which we do not. The actor was already old; 76 years in 1905 was quite elderly. Saturn's influence in the decumbiture was not good; and transit Saturn would exactly conjoin Jefferson's Sun in early May, effectively snuffing out his light. Eclipses of February 19 and March 6, 1905 had also afflicted both Jefferson's Sun and Moon.

Death came with the transiting Sun very closely conjunct the decumbiture Midheaven and squaring the Moon. As Venus would attest, the actor had a calm and resigned end, with his whole family beside him. True to his natal Sun and decumbiture Saturn in Pisces, he asked to see the ocean a few moments before the end.

One of Evangeline's more famous clients was Metropolitan Opera star Enrico Caruso, who, she said, never crossed the ocean during the war years without first consulting her. Only 47, Caruso had an attack of pleurisy on Christmas day, 1920, which later developed into pneumonia, threatening his life. He seemed mortally ill for weeks. Transiting Uranus was approaching a conjunction with Caruso's Sun and Moon at the time.

Evangeline first told the story in the December 1921 issue of the *American Magazine*:

I was called to the telephone three times between five o'clock and seven – seven in the *morning* mind you! As a rule, I can put off these inopportune demands. But, in this case, the woman who called me was in a state of such desperate anxiety that I couldn't refuse to give her my immediate attention. When she called at five o'clock, she wanted to know whether the sick man was going to die. I looked up the matter and told her that he would not die of that illness. Then I went back to bed; but at six I was called again, only to hear the same question. All I could do was to repeat what I had said before. But at seven she called a third time, and asked me again if he was going to die!

And again I said, "He won't die now. Not from this illness."

"But Miss Adams," she cried, "he *is* dying! The doctors have given up hope and the priests are administering the final sacrament. He's dying!"

I wanted to say, "Well, if you are so sure he is dying, why do you ask me?" But of course, I realized her state of mind, so I simply repeated, "He won't die now! He will come through this attack."

Caruso did in fact recover and returned to Naples the following summer. In April of 1921, Uranus actually conjoined both Caruso's Sun and Moon, turning retrograde closely conjunct them in June: he suffered a relapse.

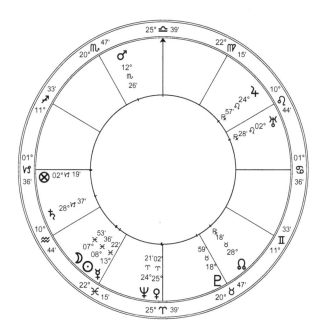

Enrico Caruso
February 27, 1873 2:10 AM GMT
Naples, Italy 40N51 14E17
Source: *Astrodatabank* cites a birth record and rates this "AA" data.

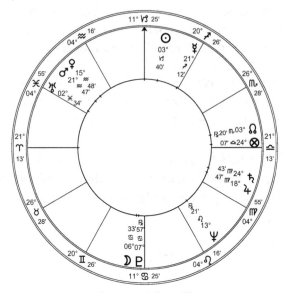

Caruso Taken Ill
December 25, 1920 12:30 PM EST
New York, NY 40N43 74W00
Source: Date and time from Caruso letter in *The Great Caruso* by Michael Scott.

In July, the same person that had called me up that morning last winter again consulted me about the famous singer. I told her then that I doubted if he would ever sing again, and that he was likely to die suddenly at any time. He did die within two weeks.

Uranus would exactly conjoin Caruso's Sun (p. 131), the ruler of his eighth house, on August 7: he died on August 2. Although the transiting indicators are portentous, it's still difficult to say exactly how Evangeline formed such definitive judgments in these cases. Caruso first collapsed on December 25, 1920, at about 12:30 p.m. Adams' reference to "this illness" in her conversation with the client does suggest that she was referring to a decumbiture chart rather than a horary. Let's look at this chart for Caruso's illness.

Here we see Aries rising, a vital sign, with Mars conjunct Venus high in the sky in the fortunate eleventh. The Sun is also the most elevated planet, all appearing to be positive signs. Yet Mars also rules the eighth house, bringing the singer close to death, and is very closely sextiling Mercury, ruler of the sixth. Fortunately, Mars also trines the Part of Fortune in the seventh, suggesting that the physician was helpful in this case.

The Moon in Cancer is dignified, and was separating from and opposing the Sun as well as trining Uranus. This is an interesting example, because Adams in 1920 could not see the Moon's next aspect as a conjunction with Pluto! The Moon would finally sextile Jupiter and Saturn in the sixth, stabilizing Caruso's condition. Although it was already within orb of conjoining the end-of-the-matter fourth house, its cosmic state and aspects were good, so Caruso evaded death this time.

More equivocal is Mercury: it rules the sixth house, is placed high in the sky in its detriment in Sagittarius, and approaches a square to Saturn. Although it corroborates Caruso's debilitated condition, its sextile to the Part of Fortune detracts from the strength of the illness. One wonders, though, whether Adams was as sure of the outcome of this case as she claimed. It's worth remembering, too, that this condition would later kill the tenor.

Caruso had been recuperating in Sorrento when he again began experiencing abdominal pains and fever. Physicians arrived on July 29, 1921, and found an abscess between the liver and diaphragm, accompanied by severe peritonitis; they scheduled an operation for August 3 in Rome. The patient became delirious on the night of July 30, and his wife took him by private train to Naples, arriving at the Hotel Vesuvio on July 31. It was planned they would leave for Rome the following day, but Caruso was much worse; physicians visited and scheduled an operation for August 1. His condition quickly deteriorated; he took a turn for the worse at 4:30 a.m. on August 2, and died at 9:00 a.m.

Mrs. Caruso was quoted in *The Great Caruso* as saying that after they arrived at the hotel her husband "went to sleep and never got up." We don't have an exact time for this decumbiture, but various *New York Times* articles reported their arrival in the "evening" and at "night." I have thus suggested an approximate time of 7:30 p.m. for the decumbiture chart for Caruso's fatal illness.

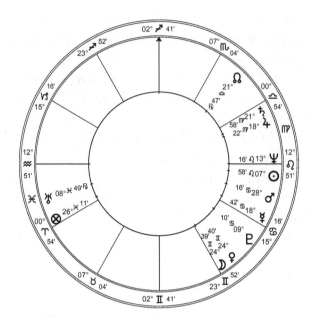

Caruso's Fatal Illness
July 31, 1921 7:30 PM CET (approximate)
Naples, Italy 40N51 14E17
Source: *The Great Caruso* and *New York Times* of August 3, 1921.

The Sun in this decumbiture is strong in its own sign and conjunct the seventh house cusp; but it is afflicted by a conjunction with Neptune, has no other aspects, and is actually placed in the sixth (the day, itself, is dying). The Sun also approaches a quincunx to Uranus. Saturn rules the Ascendant and is both conjunct and parallel Jupiter, ruler of the tenth, in the seventh. This is a strong negative sign; while Caruso had aid from his wife and physicians, it was too late. Saturn also squares the Moon, ruler of the sixth house, and Venus, ruler of the eighth. It sextiles Mercury in the sixth, and is further associated with death through Mercury's rulership of the end-of-life fourth house.

The Moon is peregrine in Gemini and rules the sixth, giving an apt description of the singer's recent trip due to health problems. The Moon is decreasing in light, has just squared Jupiter and Saturn, and is applying – almost exactly – to conjoin Venus. As in Jefferson's case,

Caruso did have a peaceful end, with his wife and family by his side. Yet Venus rules the eighth, so its connection with the Moon as sixth house ruler again unites the illness with death. The Moon's recent trine to its North Node in the eighth house is another similar indication.

Uranus is highlighted through its placement in the first house, and it was transiting Uranus that afflicted the singer's natal Sun. In the decumbiture it is retrograde, symbolizing the recurrence of illness.

Caruso had taken a decided turn for the worse at 4:30. The transiting Moon was nearly 18 degrees of Cancer at the time of death, conjoining Mercury in the sixth and sextiling Jupiter.

In their book *The Day the Bubble Burst*, Gordon Thomas and Max Morgan-Witts say that Evangeline Adams, "foretold Rudolph Valentino's death to within a few hours." This sounds like a bogus claim, and I have not seen it in any other sources. Yet there are methods that Adams might have employed to forecast the stated outcome, as we shall see.

Rudolph Valentino was at the height of his career as a silent film star when he died at the age of 31. His progressed Sun was just past natal Neptune and still conjunct progressed Neptune when he collapsed from a ruptured gastric ulcer and appendicitis on August 15 in New York City. Uranus had recently stationed in square to the actor's Midheaven, and transiting Saturn was less than two degrees from natal Uranus. After surgery on August 15, Valentino's condition stabilized, but pleurisy was diagnosed as he suddenly worsened on August 21. Valentino died a few days later.

The time of Valentino's August 15 collapse was reported in the papers the following day. He had already survived surgery and the prognosis was hopeful. Yet one look at the decumbiture chart shows us the difficulties ahead. A late degree of Libra rises, Venus is in a late degree as well, rules the eighth and twelfth, and squares the Ascendant.

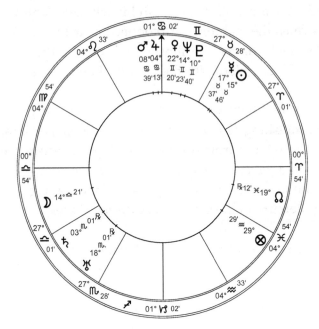

Rudolph Valentino
May 6, 1895 3:00 PM MET
Castellaneta, Italy 40N37 16E57
Source: *Astrodatabank* cites a birth certificate and rates this "AA" data.

Mercury, the Sun and Neptune are in Leo in the tenth, showing the wide publicity Valentino's illness garnered (it was front-page news for days). Yet, the Sun and Neptune are also tied-up in a powerful T-square with Jupiter and Saturn. The close Sun-Neptune conjunction in the decumbiture eerily mirrors Valentino's own progressed Sun to natal and progressed Neptune.

The Moon in the first in its fall approaches a conjunction with Saturn. Saturn in the first ruling the fourth shows the end coming right to the native. The Moon is part of another T-square, involving Mars in its detriment in Taurus and Mercury on the MC. As Mars rules both the sixth and seventh houses, Valentino's health is linked to the doctor's skills, just as we saw in the Jefferson decumbiture. Due to the debilitated condition of Mars and its opposition to the Moon, the doctor succeeds in killing his patient.

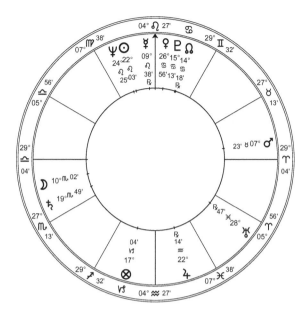

Valentino Collapses
August 15, 1926 11:50 AM EDT
New York, NY 40N43 74W00
Source: *New York Times* of August 16, 1926 gives "shortly before noon."

Evangeline would have already known from newspaper reports that Valentino had survived the night. The Moon in an angular house suggests a fast period of time; a fixed sign slows down the timing somewhat. Symbolically assigning days to the Moon's degrees, the Moon will perfect its conjunction with Saturn in about 9¾ days, or on August 24 at 6 p.m. The actor died at 12:10 p.m. on August 23, so our projected result would be about 18 hours late. Tellingly, the Moon's continuing degree-per-day journey would place it in square to the Sun, Jupiter and Neptune a few days later, when there was public hysteria and riots at Valentino's lying-in-state. Several fans reportedly committed suicide.

In decumbiture, we find critical days when the Moon squares or opposes its radical place – about every seven days. The transiting Moon would square Saturn and its natal place, then oppose the Sun and Jupiter on August 22, making this a critical day. Valentino worsened on August 21, six days after his collapse. The Moon opposed Neptune at around 1:00 a.m. on August 23. If we chose this method the projected result would be about 11 hours early. Notice that the actual death occurred within an orb of influence of both aspects.

It would be difficult *not* to forecast death from this decumbiture chart. Venus as ruler of the eighth as well as the Ascendant is helped only by a trine to Uranus in Pisces, signaling Valentino's abrupt flight from the physical body; its placement in the ninth points toward the release to a higher plane. Today's astrologers can also see that Pluto in the ninth is exactly conjunct the North Node and trines the Moon and Saturn, indicating a smooth transition.

Unfortunately it does seem difficult to exactly pinpoint Valentino's death to within a few hours, as Adams was said to have done. With all of the Pisces Evangeline had in her chart, the stories about her life and work are often exaggerated and sensationalized – and at times, by herself! Many of her reports, and all of the ones discussed in this section, were published after the fact, so we don't know exactly what Adams had forecast in advance. Yet these decumbitures are very telling, and, particularly in the final Caruso and Valentino charts, their indications are clear and obvious, even to those of us who don't use these techniques regularly.

One of Evangeline's clients was a Tammany Hall district leader, who called to ask about boss Charles F. Murphy. Adams tells us in *The Bowl of Heaven* that she told her client,

> "I see conditions very unfriendly to his stomach," I answered, after a hasty look at Mr. Murphy's chart. "He ought to look out right now for acute indigestion."
>
> "Oh, I guess he's all right," the voice replied. "He was yesterday."
>
> Two days later the district leader called up again, and repeated his question. I again looked at the chart.
>
> "It's all over now," I answered. "He's either dead or all right."
>
> "He's dead," came the husky answer. "Not four hours ago – of acute indigestion." (pp. 105-106)

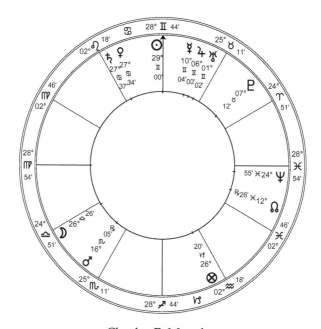

Charles F. Murphy
June 20, 1858 New York, NY 40N43 74W00
Source: Date from *Dictionary of American Biography*; noon chart.

Adams' published work shows medical astrology to be a continuing interest. So it's not surprising that she would refer to health issues in client readings. Murphy had transiting Mars in exact opposition to his Venus-Saturn conjunction in Cancer on April 20, 1924. He died on April 25. Adams must be exaggerating a bit: two days before death, Mars was at 29° Capricorn, already past the exact opposition. And it would be surprising, too, if she had alluded to death at all, as she probably had no timed chart for the Tammany boss. Murphy, himself, had not consulted her, and it doesn't sound like she did a decumbiture.

While transiting Saturn could have conjoined his Moon, formed a trine to his Sun at the time. Neptune stationed near a square to his Mars.

Did Evangeline Adams predict her own death? She died of a cerebral hemorrhage on November 10, 1932, having suffered from arteriosclerosis for five years. William Engle in his *New York World Telegram* obituary of Adams addressed this issue:

> In the starlight, her husband said today, she had read her own death. At sixty her heart was ailing and she foresaw "a period of adverse aspects and conditions over which she had to use the most extreme diplomacy to avoid the result which she hoped to avoid." For months, said Mr. Jordan, she had been under extreme strain, trying to help her believers through the depression.

Adams had some adverse long-term aspects: Solar Arc Saturn was about a degree from conjoining her Mars, and Solar Arc Jupiter approached a square to her Sun, ruler of the sixth of illness. Solar Arc Uranus was already almost a degree past opposing her Ascendant ruler, Jupiter.

Louis MacNeice quoted an astrologer who had claimed to study with Evangeline in his 1964 book, *Astrology*:

> Iris Vorel declared later that Evangeline Adams had predicted her own death and had for that reason politely declined a 21-night lecture tour which had been offered her for the autumn of 1932. (p. 198)

She had probably simply been too tired for such a hectic schedule. Ellen McCaffery, perhaps more accurately, said in the *National Astrological Journal* that,

> Her sudden death on November 10, 1932 came as a distinct shock to all her friends and admirers yet she herself in the spring of the year mentioned several times that she had no "aspects" for anything in the fall of the year. (p. 250)

But perhaps Adams had looked at a decumbiture for her own illness. We don't have a time available for the stroke that struck her after a hot bath on November 5, 1932. From her letters while on vacation, we know she often slept till lunchtime and was ready for activities by 2:45 p.m. (Letter of 8/22/31). Let's say that she took her bath after lunch, as she'd been out to the theater the previous night.

Pisces rising perfectly describes Evangeline, and her ruler, Jupiter, is debilitated by its placement in the sixth house of illness as well as being in detriment in Virgo. Jupiter is not so benefic in this case, and is departing from a conjunction with Neptune. Jupiter also rules the tenth house of outcome.

Mars in the house of illness co-rules the first house and rules the eighth. It indicates an acute condition or sudden illness and pain; in Leo it puts a strain on her heart. Lilly gives "migraines of the head" for Mars; Neptune points toward her generally weakened physical condition. The Sun rules the sixth and is placed in the eighth; as we saw in the previous decumbitures, this association makes death a possibility. Mercury co-rules the sixth and is also placed in the eighth in its detriment (or conjunct the ninth house of long journeys). Here a neutral significator takes on more ominous overtones.

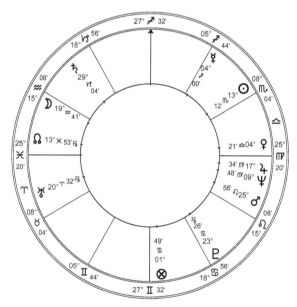

Adams Suffers a Stroke
November 5, 1932   New York, NY   40N43 74W00
Source: *New York American*, November 11, 1932 for the date; time is speculative.

The doctor in this case is indicated by Venus in Libra – a very charming man. But he facilitates the illness through Mercury's sextile to Venus and co-rulership of the sixth and seventh houses. Mercury also rules the end-of-the-matter fourth house and its square to Neptune again unites the end with this illness.

Adams' natal Uranus was placed in her end-of-life fourth house. At the time of her death, transiting Uranus in the first was near the exact trine it had made with Adams' sixth house Moon in mid-October. Transiting Mars, ruler of her eighth of death, opposed natal Mercury, ruler of her fourth. The progressed Midheaven conjoined natal Mercury as well. Perhaps most telling was Adams' progressed Ascendant conjoining her end-of-the-matter fourth house cusp. A lunar eclipse at 21 Pisces 49 hit Adams' Venus and Ascendant on September 14, just a few months before her death.

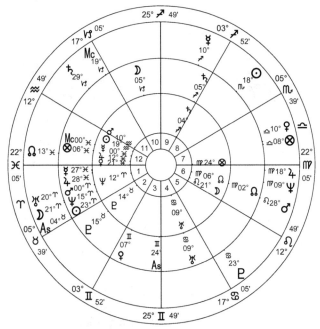

Evangeline's Death
November 10, 1932 4:00 PM EST
New York, NY 40N43 74W00
Inner wheel: Natal Middle: Progressions Outer: Transits
Source: Death certificate.

Outcomes of Political Elections

Evangeline Adams reportedly forecast the outcomes of a number of political elections. These are tricky as there is always a definite outcome to compare with the forecast. Yet at the same time, there is often a 50-50 chance of being correct!

There are many methods which astrologers have employed over the years to choose the winners; however, many only work some of the time. Dr. Broughton favored the use of nomination charts – but in several of the following examples, the nomination itself had not yet been made. The compatibility of a candidate with the U.S. chart is a good thought for national elections, though it doesn't highlight a particular year or time. Compatibility with the inaugural date and time doesn't always come out the way we might expect it. And there's always the question of positive or negative aspects – do we look to see who is lucky enough to win, or who will soon bear the weight of political office on his shoulders?

Evangeline often used dates of birth alone for her analyses – which obviously do not make for the greatest accuracy. In her published work, she repeatedly referred to general significators, which were especially useful when she lacked a specific birth time. We all know that Mercury generally represents communications and the mind, no matter what house it falls in. Venus relates to love and society, Jupiter wealth and Saturn loss. Adams appears to have used this concept in her forecasts for the outcomes of elections.

As the "Transits of the Planets" says,

> As the chief instrument in the Universe of all the ills that flesh is heir to, Saturn easily takes the prize for making trouble, and his aspects, as he slowly wends his way around the horoscope, are always productive of some form of discipline, sorrow and affliction. (Omarr, p. 345)

Saturn is also a general significator for career, as well as high office, power and influence over the long term. The only element that the following forecasts appear to have in common is that the men

Adams thought would lose all had hard aspects to or from Saturn. With her own Saturn in Sagittarius in the ninth house, it wouldn't be against Adams' nature to have "rules" she stuck to, and perhaps this was one of them.

Though we don't have very many examples, Evangeline does seem to have typically used transits to form her judgments. She may have also used progressions, easily found in her ephemeris. Dr. Smith used Solar Arcs, but I don't see much evidence that Evangeline did. I include them, however, for the reader's reference.

Speaking of Adams in her introduction to the 1970 edition of *The Bowl of Heaven*, Lynn Wells tells us that,

> In 1910 she predicted the defeat of the highly popular Theodore Roosevelt in the 1912 presidential election. (p. 10)

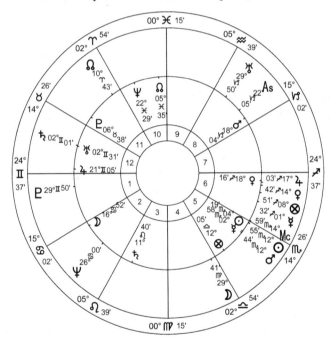

Theodore Roosevelt
October 27, 1858 7:45 PM LMT
New York, NY 40N43 74W00
Inner: Roosevelt Outer: November 5, 1912 Election Transits
Source: *Astrodatabank* cites *The Life and Times of Theodore Roosevelt* by Stefan Lorant, 1959, p. 19, and rates this "B" data.

Roosevelt had concluded his two terms in office in 1909 and had gone on to safari in Africa and to visit Europe before returning to the United States on a national speaking tour. In 1912, he had been squeezed out of the Republication nomination, but established the Bull Moose Party and ran unsuccessfully against William Howard Taft and Woodrow Wilson.

In November of 1912, Saturn did create problems. Transiting Saturn stationed conjunct Roosevelt's Uranus in the twelfth, indicating a possible upset. Transiting Uranus in Capricorn through the eighth approached a square to his Sun and Mercury as well.

Although transiting Jupiter was close to natal and progressed Venus and the seventh house cusp, promising publicity, it also squared his Neptune by the end of the month. And as Adams has said, "Jupiter is too comfortable to move the world alone." Jupiter does not appear to compensate for Saturn in these cases. Transit Jupiter was in the same position when TR was first elected in 1900, but was then supported by Saturn on its upturn, sextiling his Sun from the seventh house. Jupiter in 1912 seems to have simply indicated hard work and the expenses of a campaign.

In *The Bowl of Heaven*, Adams claimed that she foresaw the failure of both Herbert Hoover and Leonard Wood to receive the Republican presidential nomination in 1920. When given Hoover's birth date, she said,

> No one who's under such bad conditions as he is right now could be elected to anything. And neither could Leonard Wood! ...All I can say is that the nomination will go to someone I don't know – someone whose horoscope I haven't read. (pp. 74-5)

This is a definitive judgment, since both men at the time were strong candidates. Despite transiting Jupiter conjoining Hoover's Sun, hard aspects involving Saturn once again predominated. Transiting Neptune opposed natal Saturn. Transiting Saturn conjoined progressed Mars, and progressed Saturn was less than a degree from closing in on Hoover's Moon and Mars.

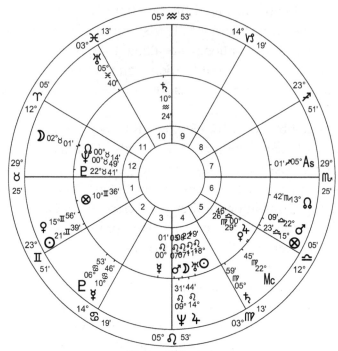

Herbert Hoover
August 10, 1874 11:15 PM LMT
West Branch, IA 41N40 91W21
Inner: Hoover Outer: June 12, 1920 Convention Transits

Source: *Astrodatabank* cites conflicting reports on the time, although they range
from 10:59 to 11:15 p.m. The time used for the chart above is taken from Robson in the
British Journal of Astrology.

In contrast, Hoover's election in 1928 was one of the greatest
landslides in U.S. history. Hoover had Jupiter transiting the first
house and sextiling his Sun, while Saturn transited his eighth, trining
Jupiter and close to squaring the lesser Venus. Uranus in Aries also
trined his Moon and Mars.

Candidate Leonard Wood had been the commanding officer of the
Rough Riders and as a friend of Teddy Roosevelt was thought to have
good chances in 1920. (Adams often referred to her *Who's Who*, so she
probably only had birth dates and no times for many of these public
figures. In this case we don't have a timed chart for Wood, either.)

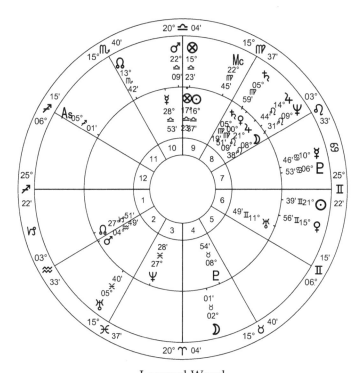

Leonard Wood
October 9, 1860 Winchester, NH 42N46 72W23
Inner: Wood Outer: June 12, 1920 Convention Transits
Source: *Micropaedia, Volume 12, Encyclopaedia Brittanica* (1989); noon chart.

Once again, Jupiter was positive: transiting Jupiter and the progressed Sun both sextiled Woods' Sun, while transiting Jupiter trined the progressed Sun. These probably indicated the travel necessary for a campaign, many expenses and wide publicity. This was not enough, however, to land him in office. He was experiencing his Saturn return, heightened by transiting Uranus opposite Saturn, as well as progressed Mars square Uranus. Wood was nearly 60 at the time of the convention, so all his Solar Arcs were close to sextiling their natal places. Solar Arc Mercury also approached a trine to Venus. All was not lost for Wood, however. Warren Harding won the election and appointed him Governor General of the Philippines the next year.

Evangeline said,

The pre-convention campaign in which Mr. Harding was finally chosen was a most puzzling one to me, because the stars clearly indicated that none of the leading candidates had the slightest chance of winning. Political managers came to me repeatedly, each time with a new horoscope. One of the prominently mentioned candidates, the late John W. Weeks of Massachusetts, journeyed to New York to consult me. In the latter's case I was able to tell him that, although he had no chance of obtaining the nomination for himself, he would profit greatly by the election. And he did. For he was immediately advanced to a position in President Harding's cabinet. (*Bowl* pp. 131-132)

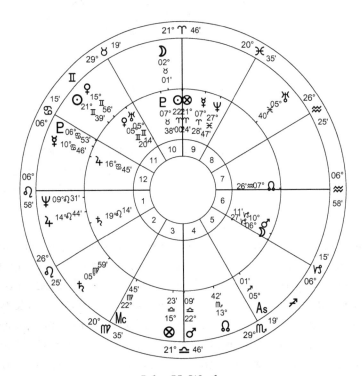

John H. Weeks
April 11, 1860 Lancaster, NH 44N29 71W34
Inner: Weeks Outer: June 12, 1920 Convention Transits
Source: *Dictionary of American Biography* for the date; noon chart.

Weeks served in Congress and was appointed· to the U.S. Senate in 1918. During the Republication Convention in June of 1920, the transiting Saturn-Uranus opposition squared Weeks' Venus and Uranus, showing why Evangeline thought he'd lose. But Jupiter would soon conjoin his Saturn and trine his Sun, opening up some opportunities. Weeks was made chief of the New York Republican headquarters during the presidential campaign, and Harding later named him secretary of war. Adams said,

> None of my researches discovered a candidate who could be nominated. Of course, no one offered me Mr. Harding's date. Most of us in New York had scarcely heard of him. But his horoscope clearly indicates his elevation to high office as well as his early death (*Bowl* p. 132)

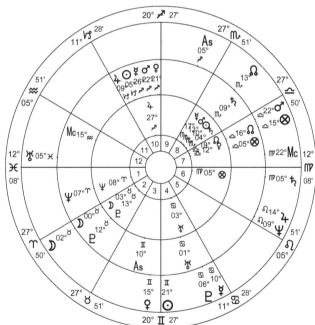

Warren G. Harding
November 2, 1865 2:30 PM LMT
Bloomingrove, OH 40N41 82W40
Inner: Harding Middle: Progressed Outer: June 12, 1920 Convention
Source: *Astrodatabank* cites the December, 1920 *British Journal of Astrology*, which used data from Harding's father found in *Modern Astrology* magazine.

Ohio Senator Warren Harding's horoscope, with Ascendant-ruler Jupiter placed in the tenth house in Sagittarius, promised high office. And no hard Saturn aspects marred his chances in 1920. At the time of the convention in June, Saturn approached a sextile to Harding's Sun. Jupiter would trine natal Jupiter in the tenth house in August, and trine and sextile his Sun-Moon opposition that fall. Saturn passed into his seventh house before the election in November. Uranus neared a trine to the Sun.

The progressions were similarly promising: Mercury conjoined natal Jupiter, with Venus and Mars just over the Midheaven. But the progressed Sun approached a square to Neptune, mirroring a Neptune to natal Sun transit. Progressed Saturn was within about a half of a degree of conjoining Harding's Sun – this seems an exception to Evangeline's "rule" about Saturn. If she had read his chart, would she have selected him for office? We can't be sure. With this conjunction in his birth chart, however, the slow approach of the exact progression indicated his climb to prominence.

When Evangeline promised in June of 1923 that President Harding was "under particularly good planetary influence with consequent benefit to the nation," (*New York Telegram* 2/4/30) she must have been alluding to Jupiter's conjunction with his Sun, stationing within about a degree of orb. Yet she overlooked the fact that both were in the president's eighth house! Harding died unexpectedly on August 2. Uranus was transiting his first house, near a trine to natal eighth house Mercury, and transiting Neptune squared the same point from the sixth. Apparently, she had not foreseen, as she'd said in *The Bowl of Heaven*, just how "early" the president's early death would be!

Adams may still have been right about the "consequent benefit to the nation." By the spring of 1923, rumors of scandal were beginning and the first investigations into Teapot-Dome had begun. The transiting and progressed indicators involving Neptune had their say. The many scandals of Harding's administration were revealed only after his death, and some of his appointees would serve prison terms for fraud.

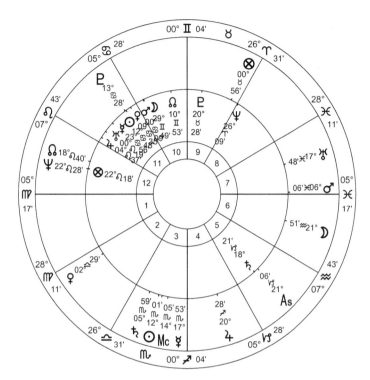

Calvin Coolidge
July 4, 1872 9:00 AM LMT
Plymouth, VT 43N32 72W43
Inner: Coolidge Outer: November 4, 1924 Election Transits
Source: *Astrodatabank* rates this "C" data, citing a *Modern Astrology* article from
October 1923 quoting Coolidge's father.

Calvin Coolidge succeeded to the presidency upon the death of
President Harding. In *The Bowl of Heaven*, Adams states that his
subsequent election in 1924 was,

> ... astrologically as well as politically a foregone conclusion. He was
> under the very best of conditions. (p. 132)

There were no hard aspects from Saturn anywhere! Coolidge
already held the office he was now nominated for, and the transiting
square from Saturn to Jupiter was already over a degree past. As
Adams said in her *Guide for 1933*,

This is a temporary aspect which may seem to cut you off from your best fortune... If you have been planning an expansion of your business, this would be a most unfavorable time to begin. (p. 299)

But by November of 1924, this aspect was lifting. Transiting Saturn in Scorpio would approach a trine to natal Venus and the Sun, and go on to sextile Saturn, making the most of Coolidge's natal oppositions. Transiting Uranus in Pisces stationed in the seventh house near to trining the midpoint of Coolidge's Sun and Mercury. Neptune, also stationing at the time in the twelfth, was past squaring Coolidge's Pluto, but Adams wouldn't have known this, only seeing that it was near a trine to natal Neptune.

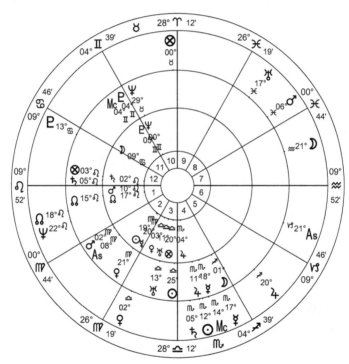

Theodore Roosevelt, Jr.
September 12, 1887 2:15 AM EST
Oyster Bay, NY 40N52 73W32
Inner: Roosevelt Middle: Progressed Outer: Nov. 4, 1924 Election Transits
Source: Sylvia Jukes Morris in *Edith Kermit Roosevelt*
cites Theodore Roosevelt's letters for both date and time.

Most people thought young Teddy Roosevelt would win the race for Governor of New York against the incumbent Al Smith in 1924. Adams says that,

> The margin between the two men was a narrow one, but astrology was absolutely certain of the result because Mr. Roosevelt was under the very worst conditions that will afflict his horoscope for 21 years. He never had a chance of winning that particular campaign for the office which his father had so ably filled. (*Bowl* p. 132)

The key once again seems to be Saturn. Although transiting Saturn would soon trine Roosevelt's Moon, it had conjoined natal Jupiter and would soon square first house Mars, both rather depressing influences. Jupiter was transiting Roosevelt's fifth house that November, but was squaring his Sun and Mercury as well. Uranus was stationing close to an opposition of the candidate's Sun from the eighth house.

Adams' reference to 21 years is also indicative of Saturn. Evangeline's teacher Catherine Thompson typically used Saturn transits as a rough guide to periods of difficulty in the coming years, as we can see in her chart analysis on page 207. Saturn crossed the bottom of Roosevelt's chart in 1924. 21 years later it would fall in his twelfth house and pass through what Grant Lewi called a period of obscurity. The cycles of Uranus overlap those of Saturn, so 21 years later Uranus would be in mid Gemini, squaring its position 21 years before and again squaring Roosevelt's Sun.

Here it's clear that Adams focused her energies on transits. She did a lot of consulting work and would have been quite familiar with the coming placements and aspects. Roosevelt's progressions looked good: the progressed Ascendant sextiled the Moon, and the progressed Midheaven had recently trined Venus (though progressed Saturn crept closer to the candidate's Ascendant). The Solar Arcs, too, were not bad, with Venus just past trining the Moon and Uranus sextiling both his Sun and Mercury. However none of these overruled a less than stellar natal chart and tough transiting influences; Roosevelt lost the election.

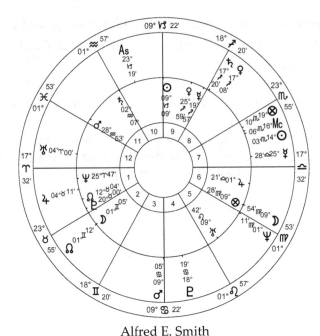

Alfred E. Smith
December 30, 1873 New York, NY 40N43 74W00
Inner: Smith Outer: November 6, 1928 Election Transits
Source: *Current Biography*; noon chart.

Our last example reinforces the idea that Adams had a "Saturn rule" for judging political elections. James Holden in *A History of Horoscopic Astrology* says that she,

     ...had a notable failure in 1928 when she predicted that Alfred E. Smith (1873-1944) would win the presidential election. (p. 214)

Smith had served as governor of New York from 1919 to 1920 and again from 1923 to 1928. When he ran against Herbert Hoover for the U.S. presidency in 1928, there were no heavy afflictions from transiting Saturn (though it conjoined natal Mercury). Transiting Jupiter did square natal Saturn, but most astrologers would not consider this that much of an affliction. Jupiter was retrograding away from a trine to the governor's Sun, but Neptune was near a station that opposed his Mars. It's hard to see why Evangeline chose Smith as the winner over Hoover, but we've lost her original forecast and she likely lacked birth times for the two candidates.

Mundane Forecasting

Adams did not do a great deal of mundane forecasting, but what she did was notable. Though she didn't discuss this topic in any of her books, she nevertheless included her house interpretations for national charts in her book, *Astrology for Everyone*. (p. 189-193)

First house: The masses, the general state of the locality or kingdom.

Second: National wealth, banking activities and matters of revenue.

Third: Transportation, telegraph, telephone or radio; libraries and public education generally.

Fourth: Mines, agriculture, gardens, crops, public buildings, the termination or end of anything.

Fifth: Ambassadors, banquets, theaters and education.

Sixth: The working classes (the masses and those who serve), industries, public health and sanitation.

Seventh: Foreign relations, peace, war and international relationships.

Eighth: Death of national rulers and matters that may be involved because of such deaths.

Ninth: Churches, lawsuits, shipping, cables and the findings of science.

Tenth: The upper classes or those in power and authority, rulers, presidents, kings and dictators.

Eleventh: Counselors, associates or allies of the nation.

Twelfth: Prisons, hospitals and asylums and matters pertaining to them.

After the publicity she had garnered as a result of the Windsor Hotel Fire, Evangeline was able to reach a wider audience when her forecast for New York City was published in the *New York Journal* on April 30, 1899. William Randolph Hearst's *Journal* was a sensationalist tabloid, constantly seeking dramatic stories to keep readers from its rival, Pulitzer's *World*. Evangeline's forecast must have served them well.

The forecast is reminiscent of traditional almanacs, as it presages difficult weather conditions, disease, fire, war and other disasters. Those familiar with Adams' later writings will be surprised at the strong language promising doom and gloom. This was still the nineteenth century, after all! Epidemics, fires and shipwrecks were much more common than they are today. Yet Evangeline is careful to equivocate. She begins and ends by promising many benefits for New York City.

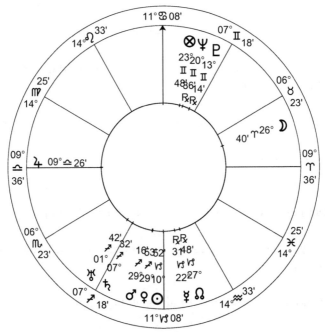

Greater New York
January 1, 1898 12:01 AM EST
New York, NY 40N43 74W00
Source: *Horoscopes of U.S. States and Cities* by Carolyn R. Dodson.

Greater New York was created on January 1, 1898, when Manhattan officially merged with Brooklyn, the Bronx, Queens and Staten Island. Evangeline's predictions are based on this consolidation date. Although she was always publicity conscious, she would never again publish such a detailed forecast. I have added the actual events that followed in italics.

THE HOROSCOPE OF GREATER NEW YORK

TERRIBLE FIRES, UNPARALLELED CELESTIAL DISPLAY. THEN SWALLOWED UP BY EARTHQUAKE.

By Evangelina Adams. Who Foretold the Windsor Hotel Fire.

Miss Evangelina S. Adams, the fashionable astrologer, became suddenly famous by her remarkable prediction of the Windsor Hotel fire. The ill-fated proprietor, Warren Leland, confirmed the story before his death. He expressed the greatest confidence in Miss Adams and her reading of the stars.

Miss Adams has cast the horoscope and written a prophecy of Greater New York for the *Sunday Journal*.

The Horoscope of Greater New York shows a marvelous future for the city. The zodiacal sign Libra, or the Scales, symbolical of Justice, was rising, with the mighty Jupiter posited therein, when the new consolidated city was born. Libra is ruled by Venus, and Jupiter and Venus are what astrologers term "benefics" – that is, beneficent planets. Jupiter rules wealth, and his influence brings power. Venus rules pleasure and the amenities of life. Their joint influence foretells for Greater New York a long era of progress in population, wealth and the arts.

It is as easy to cast a horoscope of a city as of an individual. The date of the incorporation of a new city, or the consolidation of a united one, is as reliable as the birthday of a child.

Casting the horoscope of Greater New York from the day when its consolidation went into effect, January 1, 1898, I have learned that: In

June and July of the present year [1899] there is danger of an epidemic of summer diseases, greater than has ever prevailed in New York. A scourge of sickness will pass over the country, and deaths will be frequent and terrible. Collisions and disasters on land and at sea, with heavy loss of life, may be expected.

June 6 was the hottest on that day in 25 years, with several cases of heat prostration reported in Brooklyn and Manhattan. By June 13, Brooklyn was threatened with drought.

In June and July, there were six headline reports of collision, murder, smuggling, stranding and crashes at sea. There were none in May or August of that year.

Transiting Saturn retrograded opposite Neptune from the third house. A solar eclipse in June activated the oppositions in the New York City chart.

October, November and December will be the fateful months of this year: they will be marked by many strange and appalling events, which will stir up the minds of the people and cause a feeling of unrest and uncertainty as to what the morrow may bring forth. Fires and panics from false alarms in places of amusement, theatres and public gatherings will be prevalent. Some peculiar disease is likely to affect horses and large cattle, and great storms will be frequent.

During October, November and December, three ships were sunk, another destroyed by fire, an embezzler of city funds escaped the authorities, there was an explosion on the newly installed subway, several large warehouse fires ran into hundreds of thousands of dollars worth of damage, and a lady witness narrowly escaped being stabbed in court. In October, gamblers engaged the steamer Georgiana, and took on 600 passengers on the pretense of viewing a yacht race. When gaming began, the passengers rebelled, pandemonium ensued, and the gambling outfits were tossed over-board. The ship was soon put ashore and 36 arrests made. A fire in the Union League Club in November was caused by celluloid film igniting in a picture machine. A major yacht race was called off seven times for lack of wind and the presence of fog! Transiting Uranus conjoined radical Saturn in

Sagittarius exactly in November. Since Saturn rules the fifth house, Adams related it to amusements but also to speculation, as follows:

Great fluctuations in stocks on Wall Street are promised. Great fortunes will be won and lost in a day, and everyone whose fortune is small or doubtful should avoid the Street during this period. Those who were born in any of the following years, 1829, 1835, 1841, 1847, 1853, 1859, 1865, 1871 or 1877, are especially liable to financial reverses, and should adopt a conservative policy in their business if they would avoid disaster.

The Dow Jones Industrial Average was at its high for the year on September 5, and reached its low on December 18. Saturn rules not only the fifth house of speculation, but also the Sun, Mercury and the fourth house in this chart. Uranus would not only conjoin Saturn in November, but would go on to sextile Jupiter, the planet of wealth, in December. Those born in the years cited had Jupiter in Gemini or Sagittarius, so their personal wealth could also be affected by the transit.

Domestic trouble among some of the prominent families in the city is likely to become publicly known at this time. There will be an alarming increase in the applications for divorce. Robbery, duplicity, and other secret crimes will be frequent.

She is probably again referring to Saturn's affliction by Uranus, since Saturn rules the Sun, Mercury and the fourth house.

December 2, 3, 9, 16, 30, and 31 will be evil days for the city. Persons born about the middle of March, June, September and December of past years will be the most affected by the evil conjunction of planets which will take place in December. This applies not only to persons born within the corporate limits of the present Greater New York, but to others as well.

The Moon was in mutable signs on the days cited. The birth dates reveal those with mid mutable sign Suns; they should be adversely affected by the

placement of six planets in Sagittarius along with Neptune in Gemini and a
solar eclipse at 11 Sagittarius in December.

The horoscope of Greater New York for the year 1901 will be evil
for the health of the inhabitants of the city and noted for exposes of
municipal fraud. The passions of men will be stirred, and there will be
uprisings and riots in which blood will be shed in this year.

Anti-Tammany groups met conspicuously at the Waldorf-Astoria in
March and Carnegie Hall in April. William Travers Jerome was elected
District Attorney and Seth Low Mayor, both on a ticket of reform. The
highly significant Jupiter-Saturn conjunction would conjoin the radical Sun,
and Neptune would oppose Venus and Mars in Sagittarius that year.
Neptune was passing through the ninth house, and the placements in
Sagittarius perhaps relate to "passions" and "riots." This was also the year
in which President McKinley was shot in Buffalo, New York.

There will be trouble between Greater New York and some of the
railroads running out of the city. There will be lawsuits and
newspaper controversies. The city will win.

In a series of rail mergers and raids, Edward H. Harriman of the Union
Pacific battled James J. Hill, the Great Northern, and J.P. Morgan for control
of the Northern Pacific (Hill and Morgan would both be clients of Adams).
The banner head of the New York Herald *on May 9, 1901 read, "Giants of*
Wall Street in Fierce Battle for Mastery, Precipitate Crash that Brings Ruin
to Hordes of Pygmies." This was later known as the Panic of 1901.
Transportation, of course, is ruled by the third house, with Venus and Mars
therein and afflicted by Neptune. Evangeline related lawsuits to the opposite
ninth.

Greater New York will be visited by many disastrous fires the first
ten years of its existence. In 1909 and 1910 there are likely to be
popular uprisings. A socialistic unrest will assume greater and more
dangerous proportions than ever before.

From November 1909 through February 1910, the first great strike of the modern labor movement occurred at the Triangle Shirtwaist Factory. Some 30,000 workers walked out on their sweatshop bosses, resulting in the Ladies Garment Workers' Union being recognized as a bargaining agent for the first time. Transiting Uranus would conjoin natal Mercury during these years.

Regardless of the evil promised for certain years New York will lead the world in population, wealth, the arts, and fashion. It will be a very Rome of old. Many seismic disturbances will frighten the inhabitants of Manhattan. Nevertheless they will continue to dwell on the island for many years to come with the same unflinching bravado of the Italians who live on the trembling and sullen Vesuvius. The end, when it comes, will be sudden, and the greatest city in the world will sink into the sea, and Greater New York become a memory.

Natal Uranus conjoins Saturn, ruler of the Sun and the end-of-the-matter fourth house. Venus rules the eighth house of death and is conjunct Mars and opposite Neptune, yet both trine the Moon, ruling the public. In Aries it describes her "unflinching bravado."

The close of the present year will be notable for celestial phenomenon. As the sun rises and sheds radiance upon Greater New York on December 2, there will be witnessed in the sky an event unparalleled – one no human being who now lives has ever before seen or will see again.

In the eastern sky about seven in the morning, just resting on the horizon, will arise the fiery sign Sagittarius: amassed in this sign like a phalanx of soldiers are all the planets but one of our solar system, forming a major planetary conjunction which has not occurred for thousands of years, and an event at once ominous and significant. It is portentous of great and fateful changes in the world and to humanity.

On December 2, 1899, the Sun, Moon, Mercury, Venus, Mars and Saturn were all in Sagittarius, with Jupiter nearby in late Scorpio.

Clearly presaged by it is a war in which Europe will be involved, in which England will be one of the combatants, and many now living will be witnesses to it. This will affect Greater New York chiefly in a commercial way.

Evangeline used a Gemini rising U.S. chart (see p. 174), so Sagittarius represents the country's partners. Here, she implies that England is one of them. The Boer War between Great Britain and South Africa was declared in October of 1899. There are several lacunas in the microfilm of this text, but they generally seem to make no difference in interpretation. Here, however, the actual phrase could be "the west of Europe" or "the whole of Europe."

This peculiar conjunction will affect with singular malevolence, as stated above, all persons born between the 10th and 20th of March, June, September and December of past years. It will affect either their health, domestic or business affairs, according to the positions of the planets on the day of their birth. Nervous diseases will be prevalent, and all persons born between these dates should guard their nervous systems. Their vital energy will be lower the coming December, and it will take less to cause nervous prostration and similar troubles. Many of the children born under the benign influences of this remarkable conjunction will possess exceptional mental powers and are destined to become famous in the annals of Greater New York.

Once again, Evangeline refers to those born with the Sun in mid to late degrees of mutable signs, which would be afflicted by all the planets in Sagittarius. In medical astrology, Gemini and Virgo are associated with nervous disorders. Conductor Eugene Ormandy and playwright Noel Coward were two of the unusual people born around this time.

The horoscope of Greater New York reveals that July and December are the fateful months of this year, and it is to be understood that Jupiter, Venus and the Sun are beneficent planets. Those persons or cities born under these benign influences are happily fated in general, but they are, of course, subject to the maleficent combination of other planets. Saturn, Mars and Uranus are the malefic planets, and those born under their malign influences are predestined to much fatality. There are seven degrees in the sign of

Cancer – those between 21 and 28 – which are also inauspicious. Mars had entered these degrees at the fire of the Hotel Windsor, Andrew mansion and other fires in the eventful month of March. This situation always tends a calamitous fire, and especially for New York.

I would not be a Cassandra. I have pointed out the evils that threaten this city as a warning to its people. I have distinctly stated, however, that Greater New York came into existence under the benign influence of Jupiter and Venus. To an individual or city this blessed, calamities will be few and infrequent compared with the long prosperous life the stars have vouchsafed. New York will live long and be the queen city of the world. There will be joy and love and wealth and power unstinted within its gates.

Cities, like individuals, have their periods of birth, maturity, old age and death naturally. Others die quickly through accidental or violent causes. The end of Greater New York is yet far off, but when it comes it will be sudden and without warning, and there will be a second Atlantis.

Evangeline's Leo Moon loved royalty, so it's not surprising that she "conceived a foolish, almost schoolgirl affection" for King Edward VII. Lonely in London at the time of his coronation in 1902, she just happened to be at Hyde Park Corner when the King's carriage stopped before her. He smiled at her, and she forgot at once all her previous prejudices against his unconventional life. She would thereafter "think of him as the kindest man in the world." The King's Jupiter and Ascendant conjoined her Midheaven, and his Uranus was conjunct her Venus and Ascendant, pointing toward her excitement over their fleeting encounter.

Adams says,

...Lady Paget came again. This time, she asked me to write out the King's horoscope and send it by her to Buckingham Palace. Again I promised and again I delayed – for my first preliminary calculations convinced me that I could draw no horoscope of this beloved man which would be a fit message to carry to a king.

"If he lives beyond next May," I finally told my visitor, "I'll either come to see him or send him his horoscope." (*Bowl* p. 103)

Confirmation of Adams' prediction of the King's death comes from a journalist for the *New York World*, who reported seeing Lady Paget's letter to Adams in 1911, saying: "Wonderful woman! You were right about the King!" He died on May 6, 1910. Of course, we still don't know what Adams actually reported to her client!

Others had forecast the King's health concerns, too. In his 1910 almanac, A.J. Pearce said,

"If the King's physicians would pay attention to astrological science, they would not advise His Majesty to travel abroad either this spring or summer, in view of the first, fourth, and seventh of the primary directions operating this year." (Curry, p. 113)

Evangeline, though, did not have the mathematical appetite necessary to calculate the Primary Directions that Pearce utilized. Ptolemy in his *Tetrabiblos* described how to use them to forecast dangerous years in Chapter's XI to XV, detailing the doctrine of the "hyleg." The hyleg is described as the "giver of life" and is often the Sun or Moon when placed 5° above the Ascendant to 25° below it, and similar places in the seventh, ninth, tenth or eleventh houses. The malefics directed to the luminary create dangerous times. But Adams' method, as usual, was likely more basic.

A simplified method has come down to us, which Evangeline could have easily utilized herself. If we progress the hyleg, its aspects to malefics will create periods of stress in the life. King Edward's Sun in the tenth house is a strong hyleg, as it shines down upon the entire chart. But the King's progressed Sun was at about 26° Capricorn in 1910, not really hitting anything in his chart, so Adams couldn't have used this method for her forecast, either.

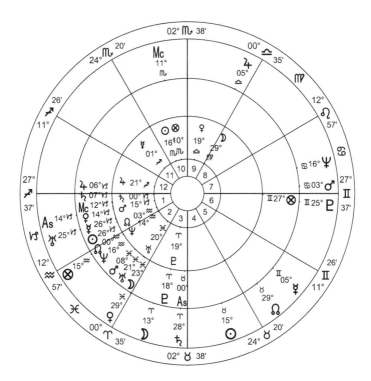

King Edward VII
November 9, 1841 10:48 AM LMT
London, England 51N30 0W10
Inner: King Edward Middle: Progressed Outer: May 6, 1910 Death
Source: *Astrodatabank* rates this official birth information as "AA" data.

Evangeline probably took more time with the King's chart than she did with most, since she was so fond of him. King Edward's progressed Ascendant in 1910 was just a few degrees from his IC, or end-of-the-matter fourth house (as we've already seen in Adams' own death), and transiting Saturn would exactly conjoin this point in May. The total eclipse of May 9 would be at 17 Taurus 43; placed in his fourth house, it closely opposed his Sun. (Although he died a few days before the actual eclipse, the transiting Sun and Nodes were already approaching alignment – this phenomenon was also apparent with Princess Diana's death in 1997.) At his age (69) the eclipse could be seen as an attack on his vitality, especially since it combined with the progression and transit to the fourth house cusp. A hundred years ago, the dangerous times were more easily fatal.

Evangeline may have also used transiting Neptune through the King's seventh house, which would exactly trine his Sun for the final time in the first week of May and potentially lower his vitality as well. For the timing, Mars would oppose the Ascendant in late April. By the end of May, Mars would also conjoin transiting Neptune and trine the Sun as well.

This was probably the reason Adams had said, "If he lives beyond next May." Still it seems doubtful that she had "predicted the death of a King, to the day" as she may have later claimed (in an *American Club Woman's Magazine* excerpt reprinted in her 1913 brochure.).

Old Moore's Monthly Messenger in its April 1910 issue projected "illness and death in Royal circles from the New Moon." In the same issue, in examining the Prince of Wales' chart, it said,

> It is not pleasing to note that Sun is directed to square Saturn, an influence which operates from 1908 to 1910... Saturn rules the MC, which denotes the father. It is therefore clear that a family loss is foreshadowed in the near future. (MacNeice, p. 287)

Evangeline tells us in *The Bowl of Heaven* that she had her own forecast for the future king:

> It happened that the London papers got hold of a prediction I had made that King George's reign would be a bloody one, replete with war and suffering; and my London friends advised me that it would be wise to postpone my visit until the British people had forgotten my "unfortunate" prophecy. I have never had time to arrange for another London season, but I suspect that if I had done so at any time since July 29, 1914, my "unfortunate" prediction of war and suffering would have "made" my season instead of interfering with it. (p. 105)

George V's reign included World War I. He became King at the moment his father died in May of 1910. Mars and Neptune straddling the seventh house cusp may be Evangeline's indicators for "war and suffering." The Moon in Aries also squares Neptune. Uranus in the first house squares Saturn, ruler of the first, showing instability.

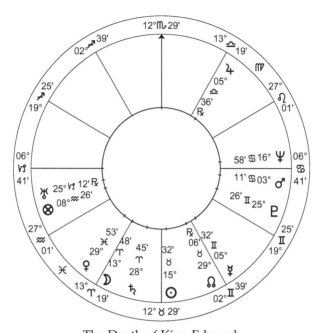

The Death of King Edward
May 6, 1910 11:45 PM GMT
London, England 51N30 0W10
Source: *King George V* by Kenneth Rose quotes George's diary
for the time of his father's death.

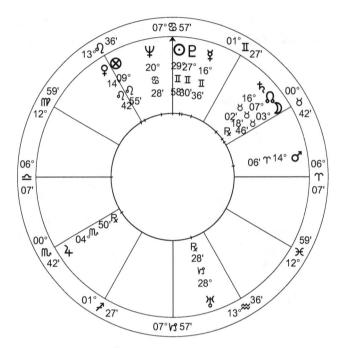

George V's Coronation
June 22, 1911 12:37 PM GMT
London, England 51N30 0W10
Source: *New York Times*, June 23, 1911.

Evangeline could also have used the time of King George's coronation, which the *New York Times* reported the day after. Here, we see a strong Mars in Aries in Adams' house of international relations and open enemies, squaring Neptune in the tenth of those in power, also obvious correlations with "war and suffering."

After examining this coronation chart and its aftermath, we'd be in a much better position to make an accurate judgment on George W. Bush's Inaugural chart. Here, Saturn rules the ninth, tenth and eleventh houses, is prominently placed ten degrees from the Ascendant, and is caught up in a powerful T-square with Mars and Uranus. Mars in Scorpio is a perfect symbol for terrorists. However, World War I was also touched off by a terrorist act, when Archduke Francis Ferdinand of Austro-Hungary and his wife were shot by a

Bosnian student on July 23, 1914. Great Britain declared war on Germany on August 4, after Germany declared war on Belgium despite pledges to respect its neutrality. Many declarations of war from various countries followed. The hostilities were overt, as Mars in Aries in the Coronation chart would indicate.

In contrast, Mars in Scorpio in the Bush Inauguration chart makes things more covert. Since the seventh house relates to one's enemies, the September 11, 2001 strikes on the World Trade Center are apparent. Congress supported George W. Bush's subsequent "war on terrorism," but a declaration of war was not made on a legitimate government entity. This focus led to America's subsequent invasion of Afghanistan and later the war against Saddam Hussein and Iraq in the spring of 2003, which did not receive the support of the United Nations. (Adams saw the seventh house relating to foreign relations as well as war.)

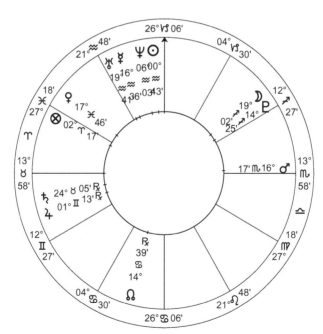

George W. Bush's Inauguration
January 20, 2001 12:00 PM EST
Washington, D.C. 38N54 77W02
Source: *CNN.com* January 20, 2001.

Thomas and Morgan-Witts in *The Day the Bubble Burst* say that Evangeline "prophesied the 1923 Tokyo earthquake to within a few days."(p. 369) We are still grappling with the difficulties inherent in earthquake prediction. Adams could have forecast problematic conditions for early September 1923 as transiting Saturn, Uranus and Neptune formed a yod; while the Sun, Venus and Mars would one by one oppose focal point Uranus.

Something big was also promised by the total lunar eclipse of August 26 and total solar eclipse of September 10. The latter, in particular, looked portentous, with the Sun, Moon and Venus all in close opposition to Uranus (there were two near-yods as well: Uranus, Mercury, Pluto and Uranus, Saturn, Neptune). If Adams forecast some dire calamity occurring around August 26 and September 10, it may have been reported to include the actual September 1 Tokyo earthquake. I've only seen this forecast in *The Day the Bubble Burst*, which I feel is often sensationalized.

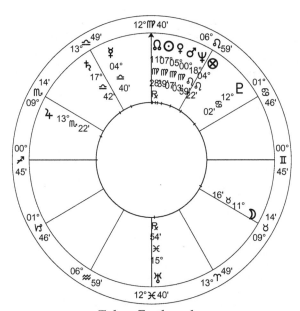

Tokyo Earthquake
September 1, 1923 12:00 PM JST
Tokyo, Japan 35N42 139E46
Source: *New York Times*, September 2, 1923.

This was a terrific quake, measuring 8.3 on the Richter scale, with a death toll approaching 200,000 and ensuing fire and tidal waves. The Tokyo water system was destroyed, all traffic suspended, the railroad collapsed and many boats sunk in the Bay of Suruga.

Japan is traditionally ruled by Libra, in which we find Saturn in 1923. Evangeline could perhaps have forecast some general difficulties for Libra-ruled countries due to this association.

L. Edward Johndro experimented with longitude equivalent charts, in which a correlation is made between celestial longitude and longitude on earth. His Midheaven for Tokyo is 17 Virgo 56, which is very close to the September 10 solar eclipse degree. (My source on this is *The Book of World Horoscopes*, p. 349, which cites *Mundane Astrology* by Harvey, Campion and Biagent, but the latter is no longer available.) Johndro's work on this topic was not published till 1929, six years after the quake. He was said to be a retiring man, and his name has never come up in connection with Evangeline Adams.

Katherine Q. Spencer, who claimed to be a student of Adams', likewise stated in *The Zodiac Looks Westward* that,

> Japan lies half under Leo and half under Virgo, but the latter constellation has a much stronger influence because their capital, Tokyo, lies under Virgo. (Spencer, p. 21)

However, she is mistaken, since her own correspondences assign Virgo the area from 140E33 to 168E20. Tokyo's longitude is 139E46.

Ann E. Parker has done much research into earthquake prediction, and uses astrocartography, longitude equivalents and eclipses for forecasting. She has pointed out that the Ascendant-Pluto lines and Descendant-Mars lines for the September 1923 eclipses cross very near Tokyo.

Yet Adams was not privy to any of these contemporary methods in 1923. Since I've never found either a published quote or any other references to this forecast, nothing more need be said.

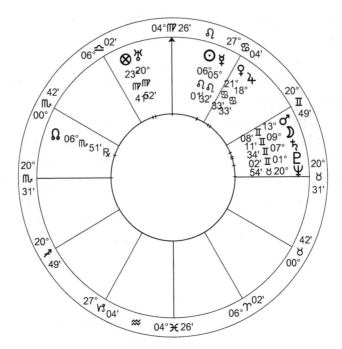

Benito Mussolini
July 29, 1883 1:10 PM GMT
Dovia Il Predappio, Italy 44N13 12E02
Source: *Astrodatabank* rates this "AA" data and cites Gauquelin Volume 5/1745.

Evangeline also seems to have been attracted to Leo Benito Mussolini, since she referred to him on several occasions. In the *Brooklyn Eagle* of April 24, 1927, she said,

> One of the most interesting horoscopes I have recently read is that of Premier Mussolini. If he continues to conduct his political policies on an impersonal plane he will unquestionably be the greatest man of the age. But if, like Napoleon, he permits his personal ambitions to override him, he will go down to ignominious defeat. The coming two years will tell the tale.

In a lecture at St. Marks on the Bowery in January 1927, Adams repeated that,

> Unless he exercises undue wisdom, Mussolini may go down to defeat in two years. (E.A. Curry Scrapbook in Winski Collection)

But in *The Bowl of Heaven* at least a year before, Adams forecast less promising prospects for the Premier, saying that he,

> In spite of his great gifts, will never attain that degree of world leadership to which he quite naturally aspires. (p. 24)

Mussolini had become the youngest prime minister of Italy in 1921 and had already established authoritarian rule. Although he brought order to the chaotic Italian situation, carrying out social reforms and public works projects, non-fascist parties had been quickly dissolved, the opposition press was squelched, and secret police had been put in place by 1926. By 1927 political observers could perceive Mussolini's urge for expansion.

Mussolini's progressed Sun was at about 18° Virgo in 1927, and would approach his natal Uranus over the next two years. But once again, it seems that Evangeline used simple transits for her analysis; as with her other political figures, Saturn figured prominently. Yet perhaps she overlooked the fact that Mussolini didn't need to win an election! Saturn in Sagittarius was on its downturn in 1927 as it transited the first house, and would oppose his Saturn, Moon and Mars in Gemini by the end of 1928, going on to square his natal Uranus in the tenth in December, all difficult signs. Yet the heavier influence of Uranus in Aries would trine his Sun and Mercury in May and September of 1928 and early 1929. Mussolini's greatest coup occurred in 1929, when the Vatican for the first time in 50 years recognized Italy and Pope Pius XI called Mussolini "the man sent to us by Providence." (Adams would also not have seen transiting Pluto conjoining Mussolini's Jupiter in the eighth during this time.)

Had Mussolini, indeed, exercised "undue wisdom?" It seems more likely that Evangeline had underestimated the power inherent in the dictator's strong seventh house, elevated Leo Sun and Mercury, and progressed Sun through the tenth house.

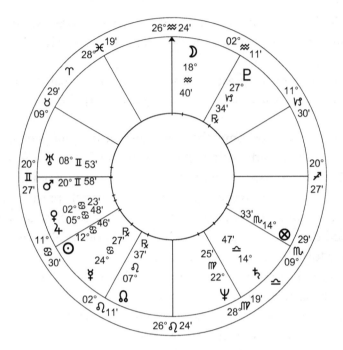

The United States
July 4, 1776 3:03 AM LMT
Philadelphia, PA 39N57 75W10

Source: *Astrology for Everyone*, p. xix. *Astrodatabank.com* lists R.A. Billington, B.J. Loewenborg and S.H. Bruckheimer's *The United States* (1947) as giving "just after 3 a.m." as the source of the U.S. chart Adams used, but there is no original source for this data. *Astrodatabank* also suggests that Adams used a 2:13:32 a.m. chart, and there is no source on this data, either. I have not seen the earlier time elsewhere, and as we've found, however, Evangeline was not one to use rectification, so the very specific time is questionable. Adams' time is also close to Laurie Efrein's rectified chart for the U.S. (2:52:10 a.m. quoted by Al H. Morrison). C.E.O. Carter in *An Introduction to Political Astrology* gives a 20 Gemini 11 rising chart, also close to the one Adams used, and attributes it to Mr. C. Hey.

The two important forecasts that Adams made during the 1920's were both based on cycles of Uranus, and both fell out in much the way she had predicted. We can see how she developed and adjusted them over the years.

Evangeline had landed in New York following her honeymoon in 1923. Met by reporters, she offered the following advice, which can be found in the *Brooklyn Eagle* of June 14, 1923:

Arriving Astrologist Sees
New World War Due in 1942

From 1942 to 1944, the United States will be involved in another civil war. Uranus will be in Gemini – where it stationed during the Revolutionary and Civil wars. The war will start in America and spread until it becomes the greatest war the world has ever known.

The *New York Mail* was also on the scene and reported the following the same day:

There's going to be a terrible industrial war in this country between 1942 and 1944... The coming war, says Miss Adams, will overshadow both the American Revolution and the Civil War and be between capital and labor, with religion perhaps taking a part. It will originate in the United States, but its influence will probably reach many other nations.

Niece Evangeline Adams Curry's scrapbook contained the next article, which reported on Adams' lecture at St. Marks Church in New York City. Unfortunately, we don't have the name of the paper, but the talk was held on New Year's Day in 1927. Adams had made some errors in her previous projections, but for the most part this forecast is chillingly accurate:

Miss Adams said the signs point to a war from three different angles: for religious, racial and political reasons, in 1942, 1943 and 1944. The same sign was in the Ascendant when the United States entered the War of Independence, again in the Civil War.

Evangeline elaborated on these themes in her 1931 book, *Astrology for Everyone*:

Uranus completes a revolution of the twelve signs of the Zodiac once in 84 years. As this planet stirs a spirit of revolution and rebellion, we naturally must look for a war of ideals or freedom once in every 84 years. It is only necessary to glance over the pages of history to find that

> Uranus was passing through the sign Gemini at the time of the American Revolution and again during the Civil War.
>
> In the year 1942, Uranus once again enters the sign Gemini and unfortunately Saturn and Jupiter will also be in conjunction with it. It remains for the future to determine just what this combination of planetary force portends. In 1943 and 1944 Mars will also be in this sign. This unusual configuration certainly portends another period when the country will be plunged into war. (pp. 180-181)

Astrologers in the late thirties were nearly unanimous in their judgment that there would be no war. Both Grant Lewi and Edward Johndro in the U.S. as well as C.E.O. Carter and the popular astrologer R.H. Naylor in Great Britain all thought war would be averted. Only New York astrologer Elizabeth Aldrich was correct, coincidentally practicing at the Carnegie Hall Studios, where Adams had lived for many years. Adams' forecasts, given so many years earlier, had probably by that time been forgotten.

The effects of the cycle of Uranus are outlined in Dr. Luke D. Broughton's book, *Elements of Astrology* (1898). He traces them back in United States history, noting all previous periods when Uranus was in Gemini. 1859 to 1865 neatly encompasses the Civil War, and 1775 to 1782 marks the U.S. Revolution. Uranus was also in Gemini from the spring of 1691 till 1698, a period including the Salem witchcraft trials (1692) as well as the French and Indian War (1690-1697). The one previous period in our history when Uranus was in Gemini was from 1607 to 1614. Jamestown, the first permanent European settlement on these shores, was founded in 1607. After several years of loss and privation, the colonists started for Newfoundland in 1614, but were met by Lord Delaware, who had just arrived with fresh supplies and support. As Broughton points out, our history could not be written without noting each of these seven-year epochs. It was therefore easy for Adams to forecast a war when Uranus entered Gemini in May of 1942. If we look ahead ourselves, we find this placement once again from 2026 to 2033, when we may expect another war. And it looks to be a big one, as Saturn will join in Gemini from June of 2030 till July of 2032.

Adams' promotional brochure, *The Law and Astrology*, dating to about 1915, notes that she had,

> In her general indications for 1912, indicated that for a period of three years, from July 7, 1912, the planet Saturn would be in Gemini, which sign rules the United States, and recalled that every war from which our nation had suffered in the past had occurred during a period when this sign was afflicted, and counseled that our diplomatic relations should be carefully handled. It is significant that the war in Mexico and the great upheaval in Europe are within the limit of this warning.

Although the U.S. had not yet been actively drawn into the European conflict in 1913 and 1914, Secretary of State William Jennings Bryan had negotiated a series of treaties which were hoped would avert a war. It was not to be, as war broke out in Europe in 1914. U.S. naval troops had also become involved in the Mexican takeover of 1914 (as in Europe, the U.S. would become more involved with this quarrel in 1917), and had also begun interventionist policies in Haiti and the Dominican Republic.

Jupiter into Gemini from July of 1917 to July of 1918 more accurately reflected the United States' involvement in World War I. The first U.S. soldiers reached France in June of 1917, with the war over in November of 1918.

Nick Campion in *The Book of World Horoscopes* (1999 revised edition, p. 408) suggests that Dr. Broughton's use of a Gemini rising chart for the U.S. was purely symbolic. In using these slow-moving astrological cycles, we don't really need to have a chart. Although it is apparent that any transit through Gemini aspects many planets and points in the U.S. chart Evangeline used, once we have defined the cyclic influence we have all we need to forecast for the future. Note that Saturn was also in Gemini from May of 1942 to June of 1944. (U.S. involvement in World War II was stepped up as MacArthur was named commander of the allied forces in the South Pacific in March of 1942 and Eisenhower commander of U.S. forces in Europe in June. The Manhattan Project was begun in June of 1942 as well. D-day occurred on June 6, 1944, only two weeks before Saturn would enter Cancer!) Saturn was again in Gemini from June of 1971 to July of 1973 (the Pentagon Papers revealing the history of the United States' involvement in Vietnam were leaked in June of 1971; a peace settlement providing for the withdrawal of U.S. forces from Vietnam was signed on 1/27/73). The existence of Nixon's tapes was revealed in July of 1973, beginning his long struggle with Watergate prosecutors

Saturn was again in the sign of Gemini from April of 2001 to early June of 2003. The World Trade Center attacks occurred on September 11, 2001, with the U.S. initiating its response on Afghanistan on October 2, 2001. On March 19, 2003, American troops executed their first strike against Iraq, and on May 1, with Saturn in Gemini for less than a month more, President George W. Bush announced the end of major military operations in Iraq.

Adams utilized a variation on the Uranus cycle for her forecast of financial problems for the United States from 1927 to 1929. Here is another report from her St. Marks lecture of January 1, 1927:

> "Beginning with 1927," Miss Adams continued, "with the influences more pronounced in 1928 and 1929, Uranus will be more unfortunate to Jupiter, which rules money matters on a material plane, than in 1921. In 1907 this aspect operated with the result that the U.S. had a terrific financial panic. It behooves everyone to be extremely cautious in investment and money matters, and be prepared for this threatening configuration of planets."

Adams used Uranus' afflictions to the United States Jupiter for her predictions. The autumn panic of 1907 had occurred with Uranus in Capricorn stationing opposite Jupiter. In 1921, the Dow Jones Industrial Average for the first time in history was in the red for its composite earnings. Uranus was transiting through Pisces, and sextiled Jupiter from February through November of 1921. This aspect, while not an affliction, nevertheless shook up the financial world.

Uranus in Aries would square Jupiter exactly in May and September of 1928 and again in March of 1929, making for an unstable situation. Uranus would then go on to square the United States Sun. Evangeline's prudence in her forecast was well taken: she only identified the years 1927, 1928 and 1929, and gave no further details. We are, after all, looking at a long-term cycle, which would continue to have ramifications after the transits reached perfection.

I was curious to see how the history books perceived this period. In John Dennis Brown's *101 Years on Wall Street*, we see such Uranian phrases as "irresistible speculative addiction," "shattered market" and "tremendous excitement" used to describe 1928. In the autumn, the Dow re-grouped its thirty-stock index to include Uranian-type stocks such as Wright Aero, Radio, and Victor Talking Machine. Chain stores, General Electric, Con Edison and AT&T were highlighted.

1929 continued with "spring volatility" and "violent fluctuations," both Uranian descriptions as well. Uranus would go on to station close to the U.S. Jupiter-Sun midpoint in December of 1929 (the October 1929 crash may also have been signaled by a station of Pluto on October 22, close to conjoining the Sun-Mercury midpoint). If we look forward, we can see Neptune opposing the U.S. Jupiter at the time of the crash of 1987.

The *Boston Herald* of April 27, 1930 quoted Adams from a "well-known magazine" in September of 1928:

> It therefore behooves the officers of financial institutions and captains of industry to display great wisdom if we hope to retain our present prosperity and avert disaster. Even the individual should make a special effort to live within his means and try to co-operate with the conditions about him.

She had also told Mrs. Eugene O'Neill in April of 1927 to expect a "bad financial slump for next year for the U.S." (See p. 120.)

If we want to know a little more about how Adams viewed these forecasts, we have only to look in *The Bowl of Heaven*, where she says that,

> When people are under an unfriendly aspect of Uranus to their Jupiter, they are bound to meet with losses. (p. 111)

And in more detail in her *Guide for 1933*:

> This is a most threatening aspect for finances. During this period, rosy schemes may be brought to your attention, which will later fail completely. It sometimes happens that large sums of money are made when under this vibration, but almost invariably it seems impossible to retain it. The same tide of fortune that brings fortune, washes it out again.
>
> Frequently, one will almost put over a big undertaking, only to see it fail at the last minute. You cannot, therefore, be too conservative as to what you do in a business way, or what chances you take where money is involved, for if you do not meet with some queer and most unexpected loss, you will indeed be fortunate.
>
> The only safe course for you to pursue is to give your undivided attention to routine or legitimate business, and refuse to be interested in speculations and schemes. If you own property, be sure it is well insured. And do not act as surety for any one. (p. 298)

Similar effects would occur on a larger scale in a mundane chart.

Gordon Thomas and Max Morgan-Witts in *The Day the Bubble Burst* describe Adams' activities and forecasts during 1928 and 1929. I don't like to trust the accuracy of this book, as the authors sensationalize both Evangeline and astrology. They do not offer footnotes when quoting text, but only provide a long list of sources for each chapter. After searching a number of their sources, I have been unable to confirm them! Yet the authors credit over a dozen researchers who scanned newspapers and magazines across the country. In addition, they had access to many personal papers and conducted interviews. So I'm willing to admit that the *Bubble Burst* team could have found information that was not available to me.

Adams did not usually call the day-to-day fluctuations of the market. Many businessmen came to her seeking this information, but she never pretended to give it to anyone, advising instead on the larger sweeps in particular areas such as in oil, railroads, utilities, commodities, etc. J.P. Morgan was said to have consulted her regarding the "long pull," i.e., the next five years, which she happily provided. She also claimed never to give specific information on particular stocks:

> When a man comes to me for advice on the stock market... I find out first of all whether the stars indicate that he's likely to be fortunate in speculative transactions. If he is, I tell him the periods that ought to be most propitious for such operations and the kinds of stocks in which he is likely to be most successful. I also give him the benefit of astrology's knowledge of general conditions, the big swings and curves – and then I stop. But I never try to make day-to-day predictions on the market's course. I leave that for those who have not had any astrological advantages!
>
> If, however, my visitor has a horoscope like my own, indicating that he could hardly expect to be successful in stock speculation or any other game of chance, I give him the same advice that I give myself – "Leave the stock market alone." (*Bowl*, p. 137)

But if Thomas and Morgan-Witts are to be believed, Adams did, indeed, give out more information during 1929. The authors claim that on February 15, 1929, she informed clients that,

> Call money would soon climb, and that a "violent upswing" was indicated around the end of the month. (Thomas p. 71)

The market had been down from February 1 through February 15, but it picked up for the next two weeks. And there were many positive transit-to-transit aspects. The Sun sextiled Jupiter by the end of the month, and Mars would sextile Neptune. A grand trine was formed by Venus, Saturn and Neptune, with Mars making it a kite. The wide addition of Mercury in Aquarius and the Moon in Libra on February 25 and 26 would nearly create a grand hexagram, or Star of

David pattern. Although Mars was approaching a close opposition to Saturn, the trines and sextiles diffused it into more productive areas. Thomas and Morgan-Witts go on to say that,

> Evangeline's fame rocketed in May [1929] when she predicted that month's market breaks with uncanny accuracy. The tabloids hailed her as "the wonder of Wall Street" and "the stock market's seer." (Thomas p. 206)

But they don't provide us with any more details until referring to a radio forecast Adams made on September 2, 1929:

> Late in the afternoon on Labor Day a reporter from WJZ, NBC's New York flagship station, telephoned astrologer Evangeline Adams for an offbeat view of the stock market in the coming months. She briskly replied that "the Dow Jones could climb to Heaven." (Thomas p. 274)

The Sun was approaching a square to Jupiter at the time, but would be near a trine by month's end: both signified expansion. Once again, there is almost a Star of David formed when the Moon enters Aquarius mid-month, offering a propitious sign. Evangeline's forecast was correct, as record sales were set on September 3, when the market reached its high point. *The Day the Bubble Burst* continues:

> Late Thursday evening, astrologer Evangeline Adams abandoned private consultations in favor of mass sessions in the waiting room of her studio over Carnegie Hall. It was the only way she could cope with the long line of clients waiting to hear her next prediction for the market.
>
> 24 hours before, whether by canny deduction or some more extraordinary force, Evangeline had foreseen the Crash with amazing accuracy, even pinpointing the pre-noon period as its peak.
>
> The hundreds of people flocking to Evangeline's studio were mostly small investors; men and women now over-committed to depreciated securities. They had met the calls for margin throughout this Thursday. What they wanted to know from Evangeline was whether or for how long the decline would go on – whether they should continue to commit the capital and collateral they still had in order to hold their stocks in the expectation of a rise. (Thomas p. 379)

If Adams had indeed "pinpointed the pre-noon period as its peak," then I am at a loss to see how she did so. There were no exact transiting aspects during the business day on October 24: the Sun conjoined the Midheaven at about 11:30 a.m., which might have signaled greater activity; Mars in Scorpio might activate the market even more, but it would not reach the Midheaven till about 12:30.

Adams claimed never to predict daily fluctuations, yet as we can see (p. 211), Evangeline's teacher, Catherine Thompson, had forecast market trends based on the Moon's movement, and Evangeline herself may certainly have done so. *The Bubble Burst* goes on:

> Evangeline saw good times ahead. Friday and Saturday would witness a substantial swing upward. She would go no further; perhaps, like any good forecaster, she wanted to see the way the wind blew. (Thomas p. 370)

The swing upward on Friday, October 25 was indicated by the Moon's placement in Leo, sextiling Venus and trining Uranus. It did square Mars on Saturday morning, October 26, but would then sextile Mercury and Jupiter, more propitious indications. The reason Adams would go no further may have been to avoid depressing the public. On Tuesday October 29, the Moon squared Saturn, and, of course, this would later be known as Black Tuesday, with total panic. By February 4, 1930, the *New York Telegram* printed an interview:

> At the moment, Uranus is in control, according to Evangeline Adams, most famous of the astrologers who cater to Wall Street, and Uranus is unfriendly and chaotic.
>
> "It is a traders' market," the stars tell this gray-haired, soft-spoken New Englander, who has advised some of the leading speculators of modern times. "Nothing is certain. The market will go lower than it went at the time of the crash, but probably there will not be another crash."
>
> "Both the Bulls and the Bears may suffer in trading. According to the stars, the trader should buy and sell and sell and buy according to the exigencies of the day. Those who wish to avoid serious loss will keep up

with every fluctuation of the market. It is no time to invest for profit. Uranus bodes no good for the man who hopes to recoup in Wall Street."

During the October market crash Miss Adams had the most trying time of her career, she said, for all day and all night frenzied speculators sought her advice.

Adams was once again correct. By October of 1930, the Dow had slipped below the 1929 low, to bottom out in December. There was no further crash, only a deepening depression.

Conclusions

After studying Evangeline Adams' life and work for over ten years, I continue to remain impressed with her career and accomplishments. She made some incredible predictions and had enough self-confidence and savvy to spread the word about astrology far and wide. Though her techniques do appear to be relatively simple, tried and true, it's ultimately her focus and commitment that lifted her above the everyday world and made her someone exceptional.

We no longer know anyone born with Pluto in Taurus – and neither did Evangeline Adams, since she didn't know of Pluto's existence! Yet I think of this placement often when I think of Evangeline. She was nothing if not consistent: she knew what worked for her and she stuck with it. Adams had a deep faith and belief in the power of astrology, as well as in her own personal power as an individual part of the cosmos. She was nervy, courageous, and intrepid, a tireless champion of her beloved "science." She believed whole-heartedly in a few basic principles and repeated them almost incessantly, using them for all they were worth. Like the writer who spends an entire lifetime promoting one book, Adams never let up on astrology. As Aleister Crowley so aptly observed, "She talks astrology day and night. She dreams of it." Adams always studied, read and learned more, but much was within the relatively narrow confines of astrology, its theory and practice. With Pluto in the second house, she valued self-sufficiency and created a tremendously successful business. At the same time, she counseled thousands of clients and helped them learn a little more about themselves, even leading some to this fascinating study that had the potential to transform their lives.

Many still believe that Adams was primarily psychic or clairvoyant. With such strong Piscean, twelfth house and Neptune influences in her horoscope, her intuition was no doubt extremely strong, and she probably had excellent hunches and psychic sensitivity. Yet, I hope I've demonstrated in the previous pages that many of Adams' interpretations were relatively straightforward. I think Evangeline would be scandalized by the suggestion that her judgments were not purely the product of her many years of study and astrological expertise! Her Saturn square Mercury would not trust anything not grounded or repeatable.

Evangeline Adams was lucky enough to study astrology in the nineteenth century – a time when a neo-classical astrology was the only type available. Today we are more likely to be led astray by the myriad techniques, discoveries, new bodies and seemingly endless psychological interpretations touted by an ever-growing field of "professionals." Evangeline practiced good, solid, old-time astro-logy. She made judgments, uplifted her clients and helped them understand and grapple with the complications in their lives. Perhaps she was too idealistic. Perhaps she sugarcoated or even evaded the truth at times. But she was a true astrologer in a line of practitioners going back over two millennia. With a little effort, we, too, can follow in her footsteps.

Appendix I: Evangeline Adams' Birth Chart

Evangeline Adams was born on February 8, 1868 at 8:30 a.m. LMT, in Jersey City, New Jersey. Her birth date is recorded in *A Genealogical History of Henry Adams of Braintree, Massachusetts* (1898), in 1900 Census records, and on her death certificate. Evangeline gives us the time of birth in her autobiography *The Bowl of Heaven*, citing her father's diary.

There is no mystery to Adams' birth date. The only day and year that have ever been published are February 8, 1868. Adams consistently refers to her chart placements in *The Bowl of Heaven*. *A Genealogical History of Henry Adams* also gives the dates of Evangeline's brothers John (born in Orange, NJ on January 9, 1859); Charles (born on November 18, 1861 in Jersey City) and William (born on July 12, 1864 also in Jersey City). John's obituary from Phillips Academy confirms his birth date, as does his birth certificate. Charles' birth certificate confirms his month and year of birth. A probable birth certificate for William confirms his month and year of birth; his daughter's birth certificate confirms the year. Unfortunately, no official birth record is available for Evangeline. But since the birth dates of all three surviving brothers are more or less confirmed, this lends credibility to Adams' date as well.

Both Adams and her husband lied about their ages on their marriage license, since their 22-year age difference was unusual. The 1910 and 1920 Census records also list differing ages, though Lois Rodden has said that these are often given by the person interviewed and may have little accuracy. They could have been completed by Adams' assistants.

Adams' teacher, Catherine Thompson, wrote to Alan Leo's *Modern Astrology* magazine after they had published an 1868 birth date for Adams. Her letter appeared in the July-August 1933 issue and said,

> I met Miss Adams in her studio in Boston in 1898, and I have friends who knew her here, and we cannot understand why ten years have been taken off her age.

Thompson goes on to suggest a birth year of 1859, but this could not be true, since Adams' brother John was born then. Thompson never gives a complete birth date or claims to have seen Evangeline's chart. Supporters of alternate dates cobble together a potential year with her stated date and time, producing a curious imaginative mélange. Ultimately, there's nothing tangible to suggest an alternate birth chart for Evangeline.

Appendix II: Dr. Broughton's Table of Essential Dignities
(from *Elements of Astrology*, p. 237)

Sign	Ruler	Exaltation	Triplicity	Detriment	Fall
Aries	Mars	Sun	Sun, Jupiter	Venus	Saturn
Taurus	Venus	Moon	Venus, Moon	Mars	
Gemini	Mercury	N. Node	Saturn, Mercury	Jupiter	S. Node
Cancer	Moon	Jupiter	Mars	Saturn	Mars
Leo	Sun		Sun, Jupiter	Saturn	
Virgo	Mercury	Mercury	Venus, Moon	Jupiter	Venus
Libra	Venus	Saturn	Saturn, Mercury	Mars	Sun
Scorpio	Mars		Mars	Venus	Moon
Sagittarius	Jupiter	S. Node	Sun, Jupiter	Mercury	N. Node
Capricorn	Saturn	Mars	Venus, Moon	Moon	Jupiter
Aquarius	Saturn		Saturn, Mercury	Sun	
Pisces	Jupiter	Venus	Mars	Mercury	Mercury

Appendix III: In Her Own Words

What advice would Adams have given a novice astrologer? This excerpt from an interview with Adams in the *Brooklyn Eagle Magazine* on April 24, 1927 gives us a clue.

Modern Astrologers

I have sat behind this desk for nearly thirty years, listening to stories, some tragic, some sentimental, from people in all walks of life. I waste no words; I get down at once to vital facts. And I must say that this is a changing world. I don't mean that we have reached a better state of affairs. I merely say it is different. One thing in its favor is that it does not seek to negate life or evade issues.

My recipe for success is just hard work. I work eighteen hours a day and have done so for over a quarter of a century. I never make a social engagement. There is no game, no diversion, I could engage in that would be half so fascinating as my own profession. What could I possibly do which would be half so absorbing? The heartaches of the world as well as the hopes and strivings come to me for help. At least that is the way I view it.

As to laying down rules for aspiring astrologers, I hardly know where to begin. But this fact must be evident to any such aspirants – the road ahead is thorny and beset with many obstacles. There is still great antagonism in many circles to its practice. That must be fully appreciated at the outset. But first and foremost, it is vital that the meaning of astrology must strike one with deep religious conviction. This point is cardinal. If one is to be convincing to others, one must believe wholeheartedly in the sufficiency of his gospel.

It is necessary that one should have an aptitude for math and be technically grounded in the casting of a horoscope. Then there's the question of reading the horoscope. While anyone, with sufficient practice, can cast one, few can read one. And few should! Into the reading enters God-given qualities of judgment, tact and common sense. A good astrologer is constantly in need of these things.

Evangeline occasionally included additional astrological information with her written reports. These educated the reader, but also served to intrigue and entice them into more purchases! The following monograph from Adams was kindly provided by Roxana Muise from her mother Patricia Crossley's collection.

The Moving Picture as Simile of Life

Viewing the science of Astrology from a very human and personal standpoint, the Horoscope can be compared to a Moving Picture which starts to unroll at the moment of birth. Just as in the motion picture world there are films of the Sunny Brook Farm type, those of the Charlie Chaplin type, and still others which portray the great events of the world, so in the case of people's lives; some individuals play just ordinary parts, others play comedy, furnishing a bit of spice to life, while some are the builders of great industries or organizers of artistic and musical movements, and still others, by being impersonal and Universal help humanity to greater things in science, philosophy and spirituality. Your character, which is Destiny, determines what your picture shall be, but the great question is, are you the Star in your picture or are you playing a minor part because you have not made the most of your opportunities and have lacked ambition?

The person possessing a great philosophy, and who realizes the power of non-resistance, appreciates that it is safest to follow harmoniously the natural sequence of events, thus making the most of each picture as it appears on the screen. It requires tremendous spiritual understanding to be able to transcend what to most of us seems the inevitable, but we must try to live up to the conviction that everything which comes to our mill is grist.

The projector realizes that he cannot make his story more interesting or thrilling by showing the pictures on the fifth reel before he has shown the fourth. To make his story intelligent and complete, he must show the incidents in consecutive order. The old saying that "every dog has his day" can be applied to Astrology. Many, through procrastination, fail to take advantage of life's opportunities until too late, while others, by being impatient, act from impulse and without reflection, and unwisely force issues. They apparently may succeed, but by doing so they have interfered with a larger plan; co-operation with Fate would have brought them greater and richer experiences. The degree of success or misfortune varies according to hereditary influences, traditions, and back-ground, as well as personal effort.

In one person's Destiny, the first reels may be cheerful and fortunate, and the life start out in a happy home and with many advantages. Then perhaps the later reels will portray the domestic or business life as clouded by dark shadows and much misfortune, but these will furnish an opportunity for developing the character and weaving into the web of life a deeper and sounder philosophy.

The Destiny of another individual may start with privations, misfortunes, and gray tones. This individual is denied love, advantages and happiness in early life, but through discipline and hardship he is given an opportunity to cultivate moral and spiritual strength, and may develop into being one of the captains of industry, a leader in politics, or preside at the head of a happy or sumptuous home.

> Character being Destiny, it all depends upon the moral fiber and degree of free will one has acquired as to whether early adversities and the necessity for self-denial crushes ambition or makes for genius.

Shortly after she began practicing astrology, Evangeline prepared a sales brochure that explained what astrology could do, and described her services and fees. She had similar material on hand throughout much of her career. Her brochure, *Scientific Astrology Explained*, which was copyrighted in 1913 and priced at 10 cents, included the following excerpt.

Scientific Astrology

You may say, "I do not believe in Astrology"; but are you sure you know what Astrology really is, and what benefits you may derive from investigating its claims? Few people know the truth about Astrology; for, unfortunately, it has been commercialized by many persons possessing a very superficial knowledge of this profound science. To begin, Astrology has proved historically to be the Science by which you may know thyself. The question is how are you going to manage your life until you do know yourself? In ignorance you cannot guide or direct your life – you only drift. Your planets reveal your characteristics, now existing and potential; they indicate the cause of disease; they point out tendencies mental, moral and spiritual. In short, they tell you the path to take through life.

"Forewarned is forearmed." To be prepared to deal with a tendency to disease, or to meet an unfortunate event, is certainly a more powerful attitude than to be taken unawares, even if the thing were inevitable; but it is not; for if sufficient courage and strength of character can be mustered, some unpleasant things can be avoided, and those which cannot be escaped can, at least, be met, faced, understood, and compelled to serve our purpose in life. The forewarning of the physical and mental weaknesses to which all human beings are heir is the strongest shield we can have to protect ourselves against mistakes, for each of us is his own greatest enemy.

The results of the association of two people in matrimonial or business partnership depend principally upon the balancing of the planetary positions at the time of their births. We have all seen among those about us, two individuals who apparently have everything that should make their lives perfectly happy; but in reality they are not. Why? Because the planets under which they were born do not harmonize.

In the education of children Astrological guidance is indispensable. While the child is too young to show its characteristics and tendencies they should be pointed out to the parents, so that the young sapling shall not be ruined by a mistake in early training, the youth not be driven into a trade or a profession to which his nature is utterly opposed, and which is bound to prove a loss of time and money, and to bring the discouragement so often fatally disastrous.

The lesson of Astrology is to teach you Nature's intention as indicated by the planets; to deviate from it tends to failure, to know it gives power, to pursue it success. It is based on mathematics, the coincidence of Celestial and Terrestrial history and Law of Periodicity. Centuries ago it was universally associated with Astronomy. The scientists of old made observations and noted and recorded carefully the experience and characteristics of thousands of individuals born under the different aspects or positions of the heavenly bodies, and thus discovered the fact that the aspects of the past continually repeat themselves, making it possible in the present to read the future from the past. An Astrologer can read the tendencies in human beings with as scientific exactness as the Astronomer can figure the time of eclipses for years of the future.

There is no study older than the study of Astrology. From the beginning of history the supreme aim of human effort has been to understand the whence, the why, and the whither of life. It is said Solomon the Ruler ordered his civil affairs by the counsels of an Astrologer. Shakespeare said of the world, "It is the stars above us that govern our condition." Napoleon held himself an agent of planetary forces to such an extent that the ignorant considered him superstitious; in fact it was only when he, most famous of generals, heeded not the forecast of his Astrologer that he met his Waterloo. We are all inclined to brand as "superstitious" those who are acquainted with the laws of which we know nothing. In the Hebrew Bible Daniel declares, "Thy kingdom shall be shown unto me after that Thou hast learnt that the Heavens do rule."

The planetary configuration in the Zodiac operative at the time of birth determines the main characteristics of the person, which are dominant throughout life. Subsequent planetary transits of any day in that life will determine Fate in a degree only modified by one's will-power to resist the influences.

Appendix IV: Writings of Adams' Teachers and Friends

Elizabeth Stuart Phelps

The following excerpt from *The Gates Ajar* gives an example of what Evangeline may have been taught in Sunday school as an adolescent. Phelps' solid faith and belief in Christianity are evident. Evangeline was always a Christian herself, and we can recognize some of the ideals she must have held in this piece.

Mary Finds Some Help

I sat down by the window, and hid my face in both my hands. I must have sat there some time, for I had quite forgotten that I had company to entertain, when the door softly opened and shut, and someone came and sat down on the couch beside me. I did not speak, for I could not, and, the first I knew, a gentle arm crept about me, and she had gathered me into her lap and laid my head on her shoulder, as she might have gathered Faith.

"There," she said, in her low, lulling voice, "now tell Auntie all about it."

I don't know what it was, whether the voice, or touch, or words, but it came so suddenly, and nobody had held me for so long, that everything seemed to break up and unlock in a minute, and I threw up my hands and cried. I don't know how long I cried.

She passed her hand softly to and fro across my hair, brushing it away from my temples, while they throbbed and burned; but she did not speak. By and by I sobbed out:

"Auntie, Auntie, Auntie!" as Faith sobs out in the dark. It seemed to me that I must have help or die.

"Yes, dear. I understand. I know how hard it is. And you have been bearing it alone so long! I am going to help you, and you must tell me all you can."

The strong, decided words, "I am going to help you," gave me the first faint hope I have had, that I could be helped, and I could tell her

– it was not sacrilege – the pent-up story of these weeks. All the time her hand went softly to and fro across my hair.

Presently, when I was weak and faint with the new comfort of my tears, "Aunt Winifred," I said, "I don't know what it means to be resigned! To have everything stop all at once! Without giving me any time to learn to bear it. Why, you do not know – it is just as if a great black gate had swung to and barred out the future, and left me all alone in any world that I can ever live in, forever and forever."

"My child," she said, with emphasis solemn and low upon the words, "my child, I do know. I think you forget – my husband."

I had forgotten. How could I? We are most selfishly blinded by our own griefs. No other form than ours ever seems to walk with us in the furnace. Her few words made me feel that this woman who was going to help me had suffered too; had suffered perhaps more than I, that, if I sat as a little child at her feet, she could teach me through the kinship of her pain.

"Oh my dear," she said, and held me close, "I have trodden every step of it before you, every single step."

"But you never were so wicked about it! You never felt – I have been afraid I should hate God! You never were so wicked as that."

Low under her breath she answered "Yes," – this sweet, saintly woman who had come to me in the dark, as an angel might. Then, turning suddenly, her voice trembled and broke:

"Mary, Mary, do you think He could have lived those 33 years, and be cruel to you now? Think that over and over; only that. It may be the only thought you dare to have, it was all I dared to have once, but cling to it; cling with both hands, Mary and keep it."

I only put both hands about her neck and clung there; but I hope – it seems, as if I clung a little to the thought besides; it was as new and sweet to me as if I had never heard of it in all my life; and it has not left me yet.

"And then, my dear," she said, when she had let me cry a little longer, "when you have once found out that Roy's God loves you more than Roy does, the rest comes more easily. It will not be as long to wait as it seems now. It isn't as if you never were going to see him again."

I looked up bewildered. "Why, do you think I shall see him, really see him?"

"Mary Cabot," she said abruptly, turning to look at me, "Who has been talking to you about this thing?"

"Deacon Quirk," I answered faintly, "Deacon Quirk and Dr. Bland."

She put her other arm around me with a quick movement, as if she would shield me from Deacon Quirk and Dr. Bland.

"Do you think you will see him again? You might as well ask me if I thought God made you and made Roy, and gave you to each other. See him! Why, of course you will see him as you saw him here."

"As I saw him here! Why, here I looked into his eyes, I saw him smile, I touched him. Why, Aunt Winifred, Roy is an angel!"

She patted my hand with a little, soft, comforting laugh. "But he is not any the less Roy for that, not any the less your own real Roy, who will love you and wait for you and be very glad to see you, as he used to love and wait and be glad when you came home from a journey on a cold winter night."

"And he met me at the door, and led me in where it was light and warm!" I sobbed.

"So he will meet you at the door in this other home, and lead you into the light and the warmth. And cannot that make the cold and dark a little shorter? Think a minute! Shall you worship more heartily or less, for having Roy again? Did Mary love the Master more or less, after Lazarus came back? Why, my child, where did you get your ideas of God? Don't you suppose He knows how you love Roy?"

I drank in the blessed words without doubt or argument. I was too thirsty to doubt or argue. Some other time I may ask her how she knows this beautiful thing, but not now. All I can do is to take it into my heart and hold it there.

The next selection from the Phelps novel, *The Silent Partner* (1871), is in a more romantic vein. Elizabeth Stuart Phelps remained single and self-supporting for many years, and Adams followed her example. Evangeline supported herself, which was uncommon in her day. She turned down two proposals, and she married only after she was successful and past child-bearing age, as Phelps had.

Perley Turns Down Mr. Garrick

"The fact is," repeated Perley, "that I have no time to think of love and marriage, Mr. Garrick. That is a business, a trade, by itself to women. I have too much else to do. As nearly as I can understand myself, that is the state of the case. I cannot spare the time for it."

And yet, she might have loved this man. The dial of her young love and loss cast a little shadow in her sun today. All the glamour that draws men and women together had escaped her somehow. Possible wifehood was no longer an alluring dream. Only its prosaic and undesirable aspects presented themselves to her mind. No bounding impulse cried within her: that is happiness! There is rest! But only: it were unreasonable; it is unwise.

And yet she might have loved the man. In all the world, she felt as if he only came within calling distance of her life. Out of all the world, she would have named him as the knightly soul that hers delighted to honor. Did she love him? Garrick's hungry eyes pierced the lifted face again over and over, through and through. If not in this world, in another, perhaps? Somewhere? Somehow?

"I cannot tell," said the woman, as if she had been called; "I do not need you now. Women talk of loneliness. I am not lonely. They are miserable. I am happy. They grow old. I am not afraid of growing old. They have nothing to do. If I had ten lives, I could fill them! No, I do not need you, Stephen Garrick."

"Besides," she added, half smiling, half sighing, "I believe that I have been a silent partner long enough. If I married you, sir, I should invest in life, and you would conduct it. I suspect that I have a preference for a business of my own. That is a part of the trouble."

Dr. J. Heber Smith

The following excerpt from *The Arena* magazine illustrates J. Heber Smith's profundity. We can see evidence of both his nineteenth century interest in establishing astrology as a science that could be proven, as well as his classical background (he had early on begun a theological course of study before illness cut it short).

Man in His Relation to the Solar System
A Subject for Scientific Re-Examination

Mankind's knowledge and interests appear to move in vast spirals of centuries, and once more we are seriously confronted with the question of the truth or falsity of the doctrine of planetary influences. It is a fitting time for the concerted application to the remnants of the old astrology of the modern methods of observation and induction. It seems opportune to take up again the inquiry whether consequences are yet hanging in the stars, for the reason that the scientists of this auspicious period are freed from superstition, and are distinguished for clearness of mental vision, precision of method, unison of work, and independence of restraints of every kind, as never before.

Let the vulgar pervert this knowledge if they will, and seek to make the stars panderers to their vices, or guilty of their disasters. Only truth, knowledge full-orbed, can reconvert the baser elements of human nature, and subdue in us the ape and the tiger. Until this transformation, through pure knowledge, there is that in us all that might infect even the north star.

In the study of mankind in relation to his remoter environment, the solar system, the theologies and philosophies of the centuries need be neither courted nor repelled, though they may yet be found related to our inquiries in undreamed-of ways. Should zodiacal influence on the physical, mental, and even more, evolution of individuals become a demonstrated fact to the scientific world, it will be found so through natural laws already well recognized in the realm of science.

A preliminary knowledge, somewhat more than cursory, of the elements of astrology is necessary to guide the judgment, not only in nativities, but as well in estimating the merits of the question as to the value or worthlessness of the science itself. The astronomer is not the sole arbiter in this discussion. He is a specialist, whose strength is in his limitation. From the observatory, with enlarging vision and ever bolder mathematical propositions, he interprets the limitless spaces of the sidereal universe. But his observation of the stars by no means comprehends the measure of their relation to mankind. Indeed, the human measure of the problem goes quite unnoted by the astronomer, in most modern instances. He may, perchance, fatally mislead his neighbor in assuming to decide, from his level of vision, the limitations of astral influences.

The conviction that man is never a thing separate from the stars has become an age-long verity, as much as any other part of human consciousness, and against it the waves of science beat in vain. It is a belief that has been evolved co-eval with human reverence for the Supreme Being "that maketh the seven planets and Orion, and turneth the shadows of death into the morning and maketh the day dark with night." Science in its terms and limitations is continually changing, but such grand *a priori* intuitions continue. Who can tell whether they are not born of memories of the soul, returning from an abyss of prehistoric ages of experimental knowledge or inspiration?

Born of human interests, astrology, as known to us by the few records not lost, it would seem, was probably evolved in centuries of observation. Referring to primitive humanity, Aeschylus (born B.C. 520) puts into the lips of Prometheus the following plaintive words, of thrilling interest in view of the discoveries of modern geology and archaeology:

> But for the misfortunes that existed among mortals, hear how I made them that aforetime lived as infants rational and possessed of intellect; they who at first seeing, saw in vain, hearing they heard in vain. But like to the forms of dreams, for a long time they used to huddle together; they dwelt in the excavated earth like tiny emmets in the sunless depths of caverns. And they had no sure sign of winter, or of flowery spring, or of fruitful summer; but they used to do everything without judgment, until I showed them the risings of the stars and their settings, hard to be discerned; and I brought to light the fiery symbols that were aforetime wrapt in darkness.

The Chaldeans and Egyptians, Chinese and Indians, Gauls and Peruvians, equally regard themselves as the founders of astronomy. Does not this fact itself suggest the probability of their having received their knowledge of the stars from some common source, inconceivably remote?

Plato proposed to the astronomers of his day the problem of representing the courses of the stars and planets by circular and regular motions, and the assiduous cultivation of geometry for the promotion of their science. Aristotle recorded a number of original observations, and among others mentions an occultation of Mars by the moon, and another of a star in the constellation Gemini by the planet Jupiter. But astronomy acquired a systematic form from the genius of Hipparchus of Bithynia (B.C. 150). The apparition of a new star in his time led him to undertake the formation of a catalogue of all the stars visible above his horizon, to fix their relative positions, in order that posterity might have the means of noting any subsequent changes that might take place in the heavens. He was rewarded in this great undertaking by the discovery of the precession of the equinoxes, one of the fundamental elements both of astronomy and of astrology. His catalogue contained one thousand eighty stars. He was the first who determined longitudes by the eclipses of the moon. In the catalogue of the stars published by Ptolemy (c. 150 A.D.) which is thought to have been largely formed by Hipparchus three hundred years before, the twelve hundred stars readily visible to the unaided eye at Alexandria were divided into six classes, according to their luster ("magnitude"), from the brightest down to the least discernible. For upwards of fifteen hundred years no real improvement was made in the estimations of luster by any of his successors in this field of research. Indeed it does not appear that by any unaided effort of the eyes there can be estimated subdivisions of luster exceeding those adopted by this still esteemed and often quoted astrologer.

These indisputable facts are mentioned, in passing, to indicate that the older astrologers were not such ignorant and blind gropers as it is customary to picture them. Neither will it appear on examination, that Cardan, Napier (inventor of logarithms), or Kepler was worthy of obloquy for having practiced astrology. That the science fell into decay upon the Continent of Europe about the time of the Protestant Reformation, may be traced to whatever cause suits the prejudices or convictions of inquirers; it does not now concern us the least bit. It is the truth we are seeking. The insular position of England, appears one of the evidences of its marvelous vitality, for her laws have been ever hostile to its practice. But in this century, India has exercised a silent though potent influence in its favor over resident Englishmen. At the present time, there is seen to be a remarkable revival of interest in the science among even the most prominent Englishmen of the day – members of Parliament and leaders in the civil and military administration, at home and in the colonies. Drastic statutes, religious prejudices even, avail nothing against its brightening dawn. Again it may with truth be said, thanks to the encircling of the globe by England's predestined flag: "There is no speech nor language where the terms of the stars are not heard." They gem our most loved English classics, surviving the recent centuries of indifference and periods of efforts at suppression of all knowledge of the star-eyed science from sources that it is not now of consequence to mention.

It must be confessed that the real mystery of space lies still unsolved – incapable of solution for us, it would seem, as much now, despite the vast attainments of astronomy in its modern form, as it was in the prescientific ages. The cavilers at astral influences have illustrated science in the state of hypothesis rather than science in the state of fact. Let the ban of exclusion fall where it belongs, on mere hypothesis unsupported by observation, whether in astronomy or in astrology.

Many who hold a belief in the influence of the planets on human life and affairs are by no means certain or satisfied with much of the data available, and they yield to astrology only a provisional assent. I candidly confess that I am myself of this number. It is purposed, indeed, as the single object of these papers, to urge an investigation of the subject, a re-examination in fact, by men trained to precise methods, and who can command world-wide opportunities. It goes without saying that absurd errors and radical misconceptions have become incorporated in astrology. But are not equal blunders being brought to light, also, in astronomy, geology, anthropology, and especially in history? Those who know but one science know none.

In the re-examination of the relation of the solar system to all organized life on the earth, we require, next to a desire to know the truth amounting to an absorbing passion, a wide knowledge of correlative subjects, including the facts of astronomy. We may not secure depth, but we should take care that our knowledge is accurate so far as it goes, and need to recognize its true limits. Some knowledge is needed of the fundamental principles of electro-magnetism, the laws of motion, of energy, force, and heat, and also familiarity with the general principles of chemistry, studied as one of the prime agencies of nature.

He who lightly denies the influence of man's larger environment is reminded, in closing, of the fact universally recognized, that all life on the earth of which we have any knowledge, higher or lower, is an organic unity, with its countless activities of nutrition and reproduction depending momentarily on the sun. From protoplasms to man the symmetry of being is continued by the great crystallizing forces of his light and heat. This effulgent orb, in truth, is the very heart of being, and the little heart of man beats in unison through its supply of solar energy as long as unstopped through the "darkening of the luminary" by some overmastering malefic. The solar rays maintain all functional activities as unerringly as they accomplish the transits and occultations of the planets. And still, it must be confessed, there is but one simplifier of destiny, and that is the will of the Lord of lights.

All of the material universe, all space, all time, are one: and man, that spark struck from inapproachable light, can best comprehend the greatest from a study of the laws that govern the most minute. In the abode of pure elementary force and of cell-life, the "Koph" of the old Talmudists, where dwell the micro-organisms, are the hidings of the creating, sustaining, and destroying manifestations of the Absolute.

The piece "The Transits of the Planets" appeared in Sydney Omarr's *My World of Astrology*, and was reprinted in Celeste Teal's *Identifying Planetary Triggers*. This work had at one time been circulated to members of the American Federation of Astrologers. It is erroneously attributed to Dr. Smith. References in the text date it to 1916 or 1917, with the writer born in 1876. Parts of the piece appear to have been originally written in the form of letters. It appears to be a distillation of some of Smith's work, but there is no way to know for sure. It is, nevertheless, well worth study, as it is well done and ahead of its time – containing early references to heliocentric astrology. The style is often charming, as we can see from the description of "Venus in evil aspect to Jupiter":

...it puts you where you have to behave, whether or not, and where you would not dare to say one rotten word. It indicates fat ladies, well-fitted dining tables, gilded cages and vapidly pleasant social intercourse, in which there will not be one word of real sense, or genuine feeling. On the other hand, while it inclines to decorum and engenders perfect deportment, you will be so horrified at the realization of the ideal, that you will probably swear never to be respectable again. It enforces correct costuming, and prompt replies to invitations, as well as rapid acknowledgement of favors received. In fact, it is a holy horror! Perhaps the best feature of this trying situation is that it does not last long, unless Venus is retrograde, in which case it is best to go to bed until it is over.

Catherine Thompson

Dr. Luke D. Broughton's influence is evident in the following excerpts from Catherine Thompson's work. A comparison with Broughton's book *Elements of Astrology* shows several nearly identical interpretations. Although Adams did not study directly with Dr. Broughton, his influence can be seen on her work as well.

Nineteenth century astrologers were pragmatic. Psychology had not yet been incorporated into the language, and predictions were made as a matter of course. Note the use of Saturn's cycles in the first example. The explanatory remarks (in italics) are also Thompson's.

An Illustrated Horoscope
Showing How Astrologers Form Their Judgments

This lady was born under the planet Jupiter in Cancer, with Sagittarius rising. *A person is said to be born under that planet which governs or rules the sign rising on the eastern horizon.*

She is tall, straight, fine-looking, with an oval face, high forehead, brown hair, large nose, slightly prominent eyes and pale or fair complexion. *Jupiter is a tall planet, also Herschel, albeit, they are in a short sign, and Jupiter is in good aspect with the Moon her co-significator also in a tall sign and in aspect with Mercury in Virgo, not a short sign. Jupiter gives an oval face, high forehead and always expressive eyes, and a well-shaped nose.*

The ancients would describe her as "busy, loquacious, conceited, and apt to meddle with other people's concerns." *See Lilly's* Christian Astrology, *Jupiter in Cancer.*

She is fond of the water and of travelling. *Her planet is in a watery sign and the Sun is in the ninth, the house of long journeys.*

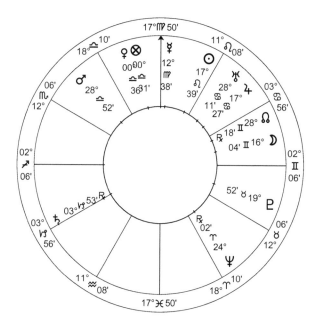

Lady born August 10, 1871, 2 p.m., Brooklyn, NY (40N38, 73W56)
Source: *The Sphinx*, October 1899.

Her horoscope is a fortunate one. *All her planets but two evil ones are above the earth and five of them are dignified by being in their own houses or signs.*

She will become well-to-do through her husband and possibly by her own prudence and thrift. *Jupiter, the Greater Fortune, is exalted in the house ruling her husband's money, and the Sun is in good aspect to the Moon.*

She has experienced poverty in her early years. *The Dragon's Tail is in her Ascendant, and Saturn is retrograding on the cusp of her house of money and rules that house.*

She will live to be old. *Her Ascendant is not afflicted and the Sun and Moon are well placed and aspected.*

She will have some trouble with her chest or lungs also her kidneys and bladder, indigestion and palpitation of the heart. *Two of the malefics being in cardinal signs will cause kidney trouble, also a fixed sign on the cusp of the sixth, her house of sickness, which also denotes some heart trouble augmented by the Sun being in Leo, and Herschel throwing an influence. The Moon in Gemini would predispose to some lung trouble and Herschel in Cancer to indigestion.*

Her abilities are very good, although she may not have had the opportunity when young to improve them. *Mercury, ruler of the mind, is in the sign of his exaltation, in good aspect to Jupiter and is on the cusp of the Midheaven, which also affects the mind.*

She must never lend or give credit. *Saturn, lord of her second, is retrograding on the cusp of her second and is afflicting Venus and the Part of Fortune in her house of credit and business.*

She is unlucky regarding friends who will prove false and must be careful whom she confides in. *Mars, an evil planet, is in her house of friends, and is disposed of by Venus, who rules her friends, and Venus is afflicted by Saturn.*

She marries well and lives happily and her husband will be the means of raising her and improving her circumstances. *In a woman's horoscope we take the Sun to denote her marriage, and here the first aspect the Sun makes is a good one to Mars in her house of friends.*

He will be tall, slender, good-looking, with light brown or reddish hair, light mustache, oval face, round forehead and a proud walk. *Mars is a slender planet and Libra is a tall, slender sign, and Mars gives a reddish tinge to the hair, also an oval face, and always a proud carriage.*

The ancients say he is "fond of boasting, is conceited, and much attached to women, but brisk and cheerful." *See Lilly's* Christian Astrology, *Mars in Libra.*

He will be a successful businessman and will become well off. *The seventh house here becomes his first, and the fourth therefore becomes his tenth, his house of business, and it is ruled by Jupiter, the Greater Fortune, and Jupiter is in his exaltation, in good aspect with Mercury. The eighth House also becomes his second, his house of money, and Jupiter is therein.*

The lady's health was not good at three and a half years of age, and again at five years, again at seven years, again at ten years, and again at fifteen. *Saturn was in opposition to the Sun; Saturn afflicted her Ascendant; Saturn was in square to himself; Saturn was on the cusp of her house of sickness; Saturn was opposing himself.*

An Illustrated Horoscope

This gentleman was born under Saturn in conjunction with Herschel and Mars in Taurus, in opposition to the Moon, with Aquarius rising. *A person is said to be born under that planet which rules or is lord of the sign ascending on the eastern horizon at birth. Before Herschel was discovered the ancients taught that Saturn ruled Aquarius, and we prefer to use it in this figure.*

He is near the medium height, rather stout, with brown hair, and a light moustache, round face, thick neck and a dark complexion. *The sign in which his planet is found is termed stout, and Saturn is a medium-sized planet, and will give dark hair. Mars will tend to lighten the moustache. Taurus gives a thick neck and dark complexion.*

His manner will be reserved and thoughtful, and at times gloomy. *Saturn gives a reserved, quiet character, and any bad aspect to Saturn will make him depressed, as Saturn has a powerful influence over his life.*

He is very stubborn and will at times be flighty. *The sign his planet is in is a stubborn one, so is his ruling star. The Moon being in exact opposition to the erratic Herschel, will make him odd and peculiar at times.*

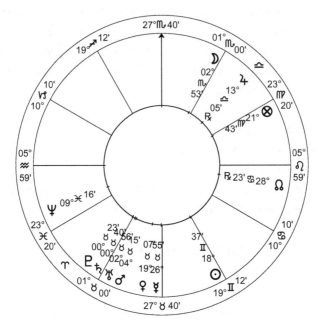

Gentleman born June 9, 1851, 10:30 p.m. at Jersey City, NJ (40N44, 74W05).
Source: *The Sphinx*, November 1899.

His intellect is above the average and anything he likes he will learn quickly, yet he will never make a good scholar. *Four planets in the third, ruling the mind, and the Sun is also in an intellectual sign; but the Moon being so heavily afflicted he will never make rapid progress.*

He is best adapted for some mechanical employment; would make a good machinist or anything where he could handle sharp tools. *For a man's business we notice the tenth house, and here Mars rules it, also the ninth, and the Moon is therein and disposed of by Mars. Mars rules sharp instruments and is in the third house which rules the arms and hands, and Herschel is in conjunction with Mars, and Herschel rules machinery and inventions.*

Those who live with him should never tease or irritate him, as he could when provoked commit some violent act which he might regret all his life. *The Moon is co-significator; being in Scorpio, an evil sign, and afflicted by three evil planets in Taurus, the sign of the Bull, gives a furious, ungovernable temper when aroused. At such times he would have no consideration for even his best friend.*

He will never be really poor, friends will keep him from poverty. *Jupiter, the Greater Fortune rules the second, his house of money, also the eleventh, his house of friends, and Jupiter is in good aspect with the Sun.*

He should inherit some property or receive a legacy. *Jupiter is placed in the eighth, his house of wills and legacies.*

This horoscope has been selected as a lesson, because it is so evil for marriage. This gentleman does not marry, or if he does is extremely unhappy thereby. *For a man's marriage we take the Moon and notice what aspects she makes after birth. Here the Moon has just left an aspect of "perfect hatred" with Saturn his own planet, and is hastening to another aspect of "perfect hatred" with Mars. Mars in Taurus therefore will describe his future wife, and Taurus is an unfortunate sign for Mars to be in. This will be modified by the sign ruling the seventh, the house of marriage; the Sun is its lord and is in good aspect with Jupiter.*

He could have married about the age of 25, and if so, his wife is dead or he has separated from her. *At the age of 25 Jupiter will be on the place of his Moon, but being in the house of death at birth it could have ended that way. His violent temper probably exhausted her vital forces, and she faded away.*

His wife would be near the medium height, rather stout, with brown hair and a light complexion. *Saturn in Taurus described himself, and Mars in Taurus describes his wife and Mars will lighten her complexion.*

His married life will bring him nothing but quarrels and reproaches. *Mars is a fighting planet, and the Moon being disposed of by Mars and in opposition to that planet, and as it rules his wife, he will be continually irritating her and arousing her temper, sometimes goading her into frenzies of rage, like the Toreador with his red scarf irritates and goads the bull.*

If he is single therefore, he must never think of marrying, and if he has married and is separated, he must not marry a second time, as it will be as unfortunate as the first. *The second aspect the Moon makes is another opposition to Venus, also in Taurus in the third, the house of near relatives, cousins and neighbors; and as Venus rules that house he could marry a relative.*

He would not have any better luck even if he tried marriage a third time. *The third aspect the Moon makes is another opposition to Mercury in Taurus.*

It is doubtful if his wives would have any children. *Saturn limits or denies, Mars scatters and the Sun burns up; and the Sun is here on the cusp of the fifth, his house of children, and the planets ruling his wives being so heavily afflicted shows they had poor health, and it is doubtful if they would ever be able to bear or raise a family.*

The following piece gives an idea of how Catherine Thompson used the Moon's aspects to forecast daily fluctuations of the sugar market. In 1899, Thompson sold her "Sugar Speculum," along with a key to its interpretation, for $25, or what would be about $1,000 today, adding that, "we guarantee it to be absolutely correct and invaluable for investors and speculators."

How to Give Judgment on the Sugar Map

In desiring to give a judgment upon the fluctuations of sugar, say for June 1, 1898, we open the Ephemeris for June and look for the position of the Moon on the first, and find her at seven o'clock in the morning to be at 28° of Libra. At eleven o'clock, therefore, when the stock market in New York is open, the Moon will be no degrees of Scorpio, as she moves a degree every two hours. And by referring to the sugar speculum, we find the Moon is in the eleventh house, and void of course; that is, making no aspects. But she is just changing signs, leaving Libra and entering Scorpio, the ruling sign of the sugar stock, and that in itself is favorable for a rise in sugar.

At one o'clock she is one degree of Scorpio, and by referring to the speculum we find her in conjunction with Jupiter, which is very good. At three o'clock, when the New York market closes, the Moon is approaching a bad aspect of Mercury, and makes it at seven in the evening. The strongest point in the day, therefore, will be one o'clock, when sugar will go up, but it is likely to weaken towards the close.

Let us now see what the world has been doing on that day. We again look in the Ephemeris, and on June 1, 1898, the Moon has passed early in the morning (between midnight and one o'clock) an opposition of Mars, and will carry the bad effects of that planet through the day, which will be shown by a downward tendency of stocks and the exchange, except in possibly sugar and tobacco. Mars and the other planets are not making any good aspect between themselves, so that sugar will not be helped by any outside causes.

We next take the Sun, and on June 1, 1898, we find him 10° of Gemini in the Ephemeris, and in the sugar speculum he has just left a good aspect of Herschel, and is void of course, as he has 12° to go before he makes another aspect, when it will be a good one, a sextile of the Sun in the speculum, and it will be twelve days before he makes it, as he moves one degree a day.

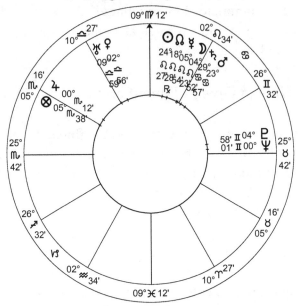

Catherine Thompson's Sugar Speculum
August 17, 1887 New York, NY 40N43 74W00
Source: *The Sphinx*, September 1899;
chart extrapolated from Thompson's description.

The next planet we look for is Herschel, a malefic; and we find him, on June 1, 1898 one degree of Sagittarius, and in the sugar speculum he is retrograding from a sextile, a good aspect of Venus, and is approaching an opposition, a bad aspect of Neptune.

Saturn comes next, and is a malefic, and is also retrograde in motion, therefore weak, but is making a good aspect to the Part of Fortune, which always rules money matters, and this will off-set the bad influence of Herschel.

Jupiter comes next, and is a benefic, and we find him no degrees of Libra, and in the sugar speculum making a very good aspect of Neptune, and approaching a good aspect of Venus. This will keep sugar up.

Mars comes next, and is a malefic, and is 25° of Aries; and we find in the speculum he has just left a good aspect of the Sun, and also a bad one of Mars, and now is approaching a bad aspect of Saturn, and in five days, on June 6, 1898, the aspect will be completed, and sugar will have a drop unless there is a very good aspect of the Moon and Jupiter on that day to mitigate the evil, because Mars is the ruling planet of the sugar speculum, being the lord of the sign ascending on the eastern horizon, and therefore has much power and influence over the sugar stock.

NOTE – June 6, 1898. Sugar dropped as predicted on the sixth, the Moon on that day making a square of Herschel, and an opposition of the Moon, in the sugar speculum, in the house ruling money and speculation, and was very bad, so that the stock was not helped upwards, but still further depressed.

To show how powerful the aspects in the speculum are, you will notice on June 3, 1898, sugar declined on account of the bad aspect the Moon was making with Saturn. But in the world the Moon was making a good aspect with Jupiter, who always rules money matters, and although this may have helped other stocks not afflicted on that day, it did not help the sugar stock. Therefore, the aspects the Moon makes in the sugar speculum or in any speculum are of the first importance to observe in giving judgment, and must be watched above everything else, according to the rules of Ptolemy and the ancients.

Sugar generally declines when the Sun, Moon, Jupiter, Mars or Saturn transit the signs Cancer or Capricorn, as they make very bad aspects in those signs; and sugar generally rises when the Sun, Moon, Jupiter, Saturn, or Mars transit Leo, Virgo, first half of Libra, all of Sagittarius, Gemini, and Pisces. At other times sugar is weak, and very little marked activity shown.

Louis Hamon, "The Great Cheiro"

Cheiro explained the history of palmistry in his book, *Palmistry for All*.

Palmistry

This study of hands can be traced back to the very earliest, most enlightened forms of civilization. It has been practiced by the greatest minds in all those civilizations, minds that have left their mental philosophies and their monuments for us to marvel at. India, China, Persia, Egypt, Rome – all in their study of mankind have placed the greatest store in their study of the hand.

During my stay in India, I was permitted by some Brahmans (Descendants of the Joshi Caste, famous from time immemorial for their knowledge in occult subjects) with whom it was my good fortune to become intimately acquainted, to examine and make extracts from an extraordinary book on this subject which they regarded as almost sacred, and which belonged to the great past of Hindustan.

As the wisdom of the Hindus spread far and wide across the earth, so the theories and ideas about this study spread and were practiced in other countries. Similar to the way in which religion suits itself to the conditions of the country in which it is propagated, so has it divided itself into various systems. It is, however, to the days of the Greek civilization that we owe the present clear and lucid form of the study. The Greek civilization has, in many ways, been considered the highest and most intellectual in the world, and here it is that Palmistry or Cheiromancy (from the Greek for the hand) grew and found favor in the eyes of those who have given us laws and philosophies that we employ today and whose works are taught in all our leading colleges and schools.

It is a well-known and undisputed fact that the philosopher Anaxagoras not only taught but practiced this study. We also find that Hispanus discovered on an alter dedicated to Hermes a book on Cheiromancy, written in gold letters, which he sent as a present to

Alexander the Great, as "a study worthy of the attention of an elevated and inquiring mind." Instead of it being followed by the "weak-minded," we find, on the contrary, that it numbered amongst its disciples such men of learning as Aristotle, Pliny, Paracelsus, Cardamis, Albertus Magnus, the Emperor Augustus, and many others of note.

This brings us down to the period when the power of the Church was beginning to be felt outside the domain and jurisdiction of religion. It is said that the early Fathers were jealous of the influence of this old-world science. Whether this be true or not, we find that it was bitterly denounced and persecuted by the early Church. It has always been, that the history of any dominant creed or sect is the history of opposition to knowledge, unless that knowledge come through it. This study, therefore, the offspring of "pagans and heathens" was not even given a trial. It was denounced as sorcery and witchcraft; the devil was conjured up as the father of all such students, and the result was that through this bitter persecution, the study was outlawed, and fell into the hands of vagrants, tramps, and gypsies. In spite of this persecution it is interesting and significant to notice that almost the first book ever printed was a work on Palmistry, *Die Kunst Ciromantia*, printed in Augsburg in the year 1475.

In examining this subject it will be found that in the study of mankind it came to be recognized that, as there was a natural position on the face for the nose, eyes, lips, etc., so also on the hand was there a natural position for what are known as the Line of Head, Line of Life, and so on. If these were found in some unnatural position they would equally be the indications of unnatural tendencies. It doubtless took years of study to name these lines and marks, but it must be remembered that this curious study is more ancient than any other in the world.

In the original Hebrew of the Book of Job (chapter 37, verse 7), we find these significant words: "God caused signs or seals on the hands of all the sons of men, that the sons of men might know their works."

As the student of anatomy can build up the entire system from the examination of a single bone, so may a person by a careful study of an important member of the body such as the hand, apart from anything superstitious or even mystical, build up the entire action of the system and trace every effect back to its cause.

Today the science of the present is coming to the rescue of the so-called superstition of the past. All over the world scientists are little by little sweeping aside prejudice and beginning to study occult questions. Perhaps the "whys and where-fores" of such things may one day be as easily explained as are many of the apparently inexplicable scientific marvels which we now accept without question.

Swami Vivekenanda

The following is part of a lecture given by Vivekenanda to the Brooklyn Ethical Society in 1896, taken from W.J. Colville's *Universal Spiritualism*.

Advaitism

Now we come to the Advaitist, the last, and what we think the fairest flower of philosophy and religion that any country in any age has produced, where human thought attains its highest expression and even goes beyond the mystery which seems to be impenetrable. This is the non-Dualistic Vedantism. It is too abstruse, too elevated to be the religion of the masses. Even in India, its birthplace, where it has been ruling supreme for the last three thousand years, it is not able to permeate the masses. As we go on we will find that it is difficult for even the most thinking man and woman in any country to understand Advaitism. We have made ourselves so weak; we have made ourselves so low. We may make great claims, but we naturally want to lean on somebody else. How many times I am asked for a "comfortable religion"; very few ask for the truth. Fewer still dare to learn the truth, and fewest of all dare follow truth in its practical bearings. It is not their fault; it is all the weakness in the brain. Any new thought, especially of a high kind, creates a disturbance, wants to make a new channel, as it were, in the brain matter, and that unhinges the system, throws men off their balance. Then come a hundred sorts of surroundings, a huge mass of ancient superstitions, paternal superstition, class superstition, city superstition, country superstition, and beyond this all the vast mass of superstition that is innate in the human being. Yet there are a few brave souls in this world who dare conceive the truth, who dare take it up, and who dare follow it up to the last end.

What does the Advaitist declare? He says, if there is a God, that God must be both the material and the efficient cause of the universe. Not only is He the Creator, but He is also the created. He Himself is this universe. How can that be? God, the pure, the spirit, has become this universe? Yes; apparently. That which all ignorant people see, this universe, does not exist. You and I and all these things we see, what are these? Mere self-hypnotisms; there is but One Existence, the Infinite, the ever existing One. In that Existence we dream all these various dreams. It is the Atman, beyond all, the Infinite, beyond the known, beyond the knowable; in and through That we see this universe. It is the only reality. It is this table; It is the audience before me; It is the wall; It is everything, minus the name and form. Take the form of the table, take away the name; what remains is that It. The Vedantist does not call It either He or She; these are fictions, delusions of the human brain; there is no sex in the soul. People who are under illusion, who have become like animals, see a woman or a man. Every one and everything is the Atman – the Self – the sexless, the pure, the ever blessed. The name, the form, the body are material, and they make all this difference.

If you take off these two differences of name and form, the whole universe is One; there are no two, no three, but One every-where. You and I are one. There is neither nature, nor God, nor the universe, only that One Infinite Existence, out of which, through name and form, all these are manufactured. How to know the Knower? It cannot be known. How can you see your own Self? You can only reflect yourself. So all this universe is the reflection of that One Eternal Being, the Atman, and, as the reflection falls upon good or bad reflectors, good or bad images are cast up. So, in the murderer, the reflector is bad and not the Self. In the saint the reflector is pure. The Self – the Atman – is by its own nature pure. The whole of this universe is One Unity, One Existence, physically, mentally, morally and spiritually. We are looking upon this One Existence in different forms and creating all these images upon it. To the being who has limited himself to the condition of man this world is what he sees. To the being who is on a higher plane of existence it may become like heaven. There is but one Soul in the universe, not two. It neither comes nor goes. It neither reincarnates nor dies, nor is born. How can it? How to die? Where to go? All these heavens and all these earths, and all these places are vain imaginations of the mind. They do not exist; never existed in the past and never will in the future.

"Know the truth and be free in a moment." All the darkness will vanish. When man has seen himself as one with the infinite Being of the universe, when all separateness has ceased, when all men, all women, all angels, all gods, all animals, all plants, the whole universe has been melted into that oneness, then all fear disappears. Whom to fear? Can I hurt myself? Can I kill myself? Do you fear yourself? Then will all sorrow disappear. What can cause me sorrow? I am the One Existence of the universe. Then all jealousies will disappear; of whom to be jealous? Of myself? Then all bad feelings disappear. Against whom will I have this bad feeling? Against myself? There is none in the universe but me. And this is the way, says the Vedantist, to this knowledge. Kill out this differentiation, kill out this superstition that there are many. "He who, in this world of many, sees that One; he who in this mass of insentiency sees that One Sentient Being; he who in this world of shadow catches that Reality, unto him belongs eternal peace, unto none else, unto none else."

Minot J. Savage

The following piece by Rev. Savage from *The Arena* magazine in 1889 makes it clear why spiritualism was at the time regarded as a science. In it, we can also see how the traditional classical view was already eroded well before the turn of the last century. Much as we saw in Dr. Smith's writings, Savage is poised between the old and the new – in this piece, he highlights the role of the senses on the material plane, and in so doing, he discounts the Pythagoreans and Plato, who emphasized invisible truth and knowledge.

A Reply to Mr. Hawthorne

I have been investigating what are called the "phenomena of spiritualism" for fifteen years. Large numbers of those who, with me, have helped to make up the Society for Psychical Research have only been hunting for something to step on. And the attitude of thousands of "educated" men is anything but scientific. They remind one constantly of Josh Billings' saying: "A man had better not know so much than to know so many things that ain't so." They know so thoroughly that it "ain't so," that I wonder why they go through the farce of investigating. Schopenhauer says that for a man any longer to deny clairvoyance, for example, is not bigotry but ignorance. Of course this does not necessarily imply spiritualism; I use it only as an illustration.

In spite of the fact that it is characteristic of our senses to deceive us, the human race has discovered no satisfactory substitute for sight and hearing and smelling and taste and touch. And it is by the use of these that we have found out how, and when, and why their reports are false. Reason and understanding are not quite independent of the senses; and it is the poor senses which supply them with all the materials with which they work. And it is the senses themselves that furnish us with the means for correcting the errors of their own preliminary reports. The man, then, who proposes to doubt his own senses must go to his own senses to find a reason for his doubt. If he is logical, he will end by doubting his doubt. This business of reviling the senses can be carried a little too far. How has it been found out that there are "bogus mediums," except by the use of the same senses?

In regard to the matter of seeing, it ought, perhaps, to be said that any one person's senses are not enough. If I saw a "spirit" ever so plainly and nobody else saw it, I should think it was probably an hallucination. But if several others saw it at the same time, and that without any suggestion from me, I should feel that the probabilities were in favor of its reality; for the chances against several persons having the same hallucination at the same time are very great.

Neither hypnotism, clairvoyance, nor telepathy need any other spirits than embodied ones to account for their facts, however remarkable. But, since they show that mind can act in at least semi-independence of the ordinary senses, they do suggest the inquiry as to whether this same mind may not be able to continue its activity without them.

If it is worthwhile to know that death is only an incident of life and not the end of it, then most certainly this inquiry is worthwhile. The world may wish, and hope, and dream, but I see no other line of inquiry along which there is any likelihood of attaining certainty. Every thoughtful person, who is familiar with the world's sorrows, knows that among all the things the poor, hungry, human heart desires, there is nothing that could lift off so heavy a weight of grief as a perfect assurance that "the dead is alive again." All the millennial dreams, from Plato to Bellamy, might be realized, without bringing to earth such comfort as this one certainty would bring. Another thing which would make knowledge here worth- while is the power such knowledge would have in helping the world to a practical trust in the justice of the universe.

It is not the inequalities of wealth and poverty that trouble us most. It is the seeing so many lives incomplete, so many crushed and hopeless, so many born to crime, so many with no brain capacity even, as yet, to care for the things that make up a really human life. But once know that endless time and limitless opportunity shall be granted to all, and this now almost insuperable difficulty need trouble us no more than the fact that all the children are not yet grown.

The old theology, while it teaches immortality, teaches also the possibility of a miraculous and sudden reversal of a wrong life of seventy years, and so has about it little of moral force. A past that can be wiped out by a prayer or a sacrament need not trouble one overmuch. And so, naturally, in some sections of the Church, salvation has become a matter of barter and trade.

But God's high revelation, through science, has demonstrated that we are under a changeless law of cause and effect, that our todays make our tomorrows, and our present lives determine the grade on which we must enter any next life. Now couple this knowledge with the certainty that life goes right on, and that we shall never, in any world, get into any more of heaven than we first get into ourselves, and I know of nothing so fitted to lift the world.

Paul says, "Let us eat and drink, for tomorrow we die." I do not agree with him, in the sense in which he means it. But if I know I am to live only forty years, and then sleep forever, it would be wholly reasonable for me to lay my life out on quite a different scale from what I should if I knew I was to live forever. If we can say with Seneca, "This life is only a prelude to eternity," then we need not worry so much over the fittings and furnishings of this ante-room; and more than that, it will give dignity and purpose to the fleeting days to know they are linked in with the eternal things as prelude and preparation.

People sometimes ask – what kind of messages I get, purporting to come from the other side – if they are not all trash? I generally reply, they are about on the level of my average daily mail. I get letters not overwise, not always spelled correctly, not always grammatical. But I do not say, these letters come from nobody, because they are not up to the level of Plato and Shakespeare. I do not really expect all my letters to be up to such a level. They come from folks. So if I can get any word from the other side, I should expect it to come from folks very like the kind I know here. Even when a man lies to me, I do not therefore doubt that he is alive. If I get a message over the telegraph wires, it may be foolish or false, but I know there is some kind of an intelligence at the other end.

And, since my interest in this question is chiefly concerned with the matter as to whether continued existence can be demonstrated, I am more anxious to know whether I really get a message from the other side than I am as to the wisdom or even the veracity of the sender. This point, then, to me, seems of no present, practical importance. If we can settle the fact of continued existence, then it will be time enough to study the country. Discover the continent first; the character of the inhabitants is a matter that can wait.

Reverend Savage wrote much on theology as well. This piece from *The Passing and the Permanent in Religion* nicely traces the history of western man's relationship with the cosmos:

The Universe

Every religion has started in a cosmology; that is, the thought side, the theoretical side, of every religion is always bound up with a theory of things – the nature, the origin of the world. It is no accident, therefore, that the first word in the *Bible* is a scientific word – as scientific as the knowledge of that time would allow. "In the beginning the Elohim created the heavens and the earth."

To the writer of Genesis the universe was a very small affair. It was a sort of two-story structure at first. There was the flat earth, either anchored in the midst of the surrounding ocean or fixed in some way in its place. It was roofed over by a firmament as solid as if beaten out by the smith from some malleable metal. In this firmament were windows for the rains to come through – the waters that were stored above the firmament – and to it were attached the sun, the moon, and the stars, to give light to the inhabitants of the earth. Above this firmament was the abode of God and His angels. This was the first thought of the universe.

As Hebrew imagination and experience grew, there at last came to be believed in a sort of basement – shall I call it? – making it, instead of a two-story, a three-story structure. Beneath the surface of the earth there was an underground world, the abode of the spirits of the dead. This may stand as fairly representing the belief in the universe on the part of the Hebrews throughout almost their entire history as a nation.

It was a modification of this which was held in the time of Jesus. In the early half of the second century there lived in Alexandria a famous mathematician and astronomer by the name of Ptolemy, who gave his name to what has come to be called the Ptolemaic theory of the universe. This held the minds of men until sometime in the fifteenth century. This Ptolemaic theory is the one that furnishes the framework of Dante's great poem and of Milton's epic. In this – to be brief – the earth was at the center; and this was surrounded by and enclosed in a series of concentric crystal, transparent spheres – to compare large things with small, very much like a nest of glass globes inside each other. To the first of these, and therefore the smallest, was attached the moon; to the next the sun, and to the rest in their order the then known planets. Outside of these was one to the surface of which were attached all the fixed stars. Beyond this was still another, close to heaven itself, and which was supposed in some mysterious way to be moved by divine power, and in its motion to carry around with it all the others.

In this way the movements of the heavenly bodies were explained in the Ptolemaic system; and these spheres are the ones we speak and sing of still, though most of us have forgotten what we mean when we talk about the "music of the spheres" or when we refer to a star as "starting from its sphere." These were real, substantial things in this Ptolemaic theory, carrying the heavenly bodies around with them in their circling motions.

Those who believed in this theory had a good deal of difficulty as time went on in explaining astronomical facts; and they had to invent a great many additions to and modifications of their theory, because one after another it was noticed that the heavenly bodies did not behave as they ought, if this theory were true; until at last the difficulties grew so great that Prince Alphonso of Castile, an amateur astronomer and famous mathematician, said that if he had been present at the creation, he could have suggested a good many valuable improvements on the theory. The inconsistencies were so great that it was very difficult for a scholarly man any longer to accept the old ideas.

About the time that Columbus was discovering a new continent, Copernicus was discovering a new universe. He was a devout Catholic. He would not, if he could help it, affront or disturb the authorities of his Church; and yet his knowledge of the universe grew to be such that he felt he must write it down in a book. Governed by considerations regarding his own safety, undoubtedly, his book was published – though I think it was dedicated to the pope – as a tentative theory, and during the very last year of his life. The first copy which the author ever saw was brought to him as he lay on his sick-bed, from which he never rose again. Had he lived he would undoubtedly have been persecuted for his teaching, as the book was placed on the *Index*, and all good Catholics were forbidden to read it.

But here was the beginning of what is now the universally accepted theory of the universe. One after another facts began to round out this theory. Galileo, Kepler, Newton, have added to our knowledge in these directions, until at last we are in the midst of this tremendous fact that surrounds us on every hand. Science, dreaded always by the Church, fought at every step by theology, by the ecclesiastics, the churchly authorities – science has at last done for us what the Church was never able to do. It has given us a universe fit to be the garment, the home, the phenomenal manifestation of the infinite God.

William Wilberforce J. Colville

The inspirational speaker, writer and medium W.W.J. Colville was an intimate friend of Evangeline's in Boston. His book, *Universal Spiritualism*, suggests he was born in 1860, and Evangeline in *The Bowl of Heaven* says that his Sun was in Virgo, with Mercury aspecting Saturn, Uranus and Neptune. Although she added that,

In private life, these conflicting influences made him a rank eccentric. I remember one night at a dinner at Mrs. Ole Bull's, Colville suddenly ducked under the table and crawled around on his hands and knees – for no good reason except that he felt that way at the time. But in his public work, he showed an extraordinary mentality, which seemed able to tap the brains of anybody in his audience. (p.89)

It's not known whether Colville used inspiration or more ordinary means of research for his written work; a sample from *Our Places in the Universal Zodiac* appears below.

Saturnalia

It is a noteworthy fact that all the feasts and fasts of the Christian calendar owe their literal origin to astronomy and astrology, and nowhere does this fact strike the thoughtful student more impressively than at Christmas tide, when the earth enters Capricorn on the shortest day of the year, December 21. Following this day dedicated to Saint Thomas, the doubting Didymus of gospel story, come the three days of uncertainty and gloom, according to the old Egyptian idea, during which the sun was supposed to be imprisoned in Hades; then when December 22, 23 and 24 are over, the sun reappears above the line on Christmas day, December 25, which is the natural birthday of the year, and celebrated on that account with the greatest jubilation, from the earliest recorded time. The Roman Saturnalian feast and the Druid's Yuletide festivities can all be traced to the same origin. At the time of the winter solstice we reach the darkest, longest nights and the shortest, dullest days; but immediately the night has seemingly gained a victory over the day; the tables are turned, and at once we behold an increase in the length and brightness of the day, and an equal decrease in the length and darkness of the night.

For several centuries the Fathers of the Christian Church were undecided as to the proper time for celebrating Christmas. Some kept the festival of the nativity of the Christ in the spring; others, in the autumn, but at length the unanimous decision was reached that it was highly appropriate to take the ancient solar festival of the new birth of Osiris, the light-bringer, and connect it with a distinctively Christian idea. Such is the origin of Christmas with all its traditions of frost and snow.

Oliver Ames Goold

Another Boston friend of Evangeline's was Oliver Ames Goold. She called him a "brilliant astrologer" and mentioned several of his successful predictions in *The Bowl of Heaven*. Unfortunately, Goold's horoscope has also been lost to us, but some of his thoughts are preserved in his 1885 introduction to the reprint of James Wilson's *Dictionary of Astrology*. Nineteenth century astrologers were classical revivalists who returned to Ptolemy and other "ancients" at their disposal, like William Lilly. Though Wilson's first edition was written nearly 65 years earlier, Goold takes exception to some of the "scientific" steps the author had taken to pare down astrology to what he thought were its more essential elements. (Wilson was ahead of his time, as this process continued well into the twentieth century.) Goold's astrology seems rather sound, based on experience with clients, acceptance of traditions such as the importance of angularity, the Moon's Nodes and essential dignities, and a healthy skepticism about the houses and making specific judgments. We can only assume that Evangeline supported such wise ideas in practice herself, since she had high regard for Goold.

Prolegomena

In the course of my earlier study of the elementary part of the science (before I had ventured to its practice), I applied to an old and quite learned professor of astrology, and, with candor, asked him some plain and simple questions for information. I received in reply no scrap of knowledge, but met with the discouragement of his assumption that he could do what no one else could, in the application of planetary laws. He appeared anxious to shroud the subject in mystery, and to claim special inspiration necessary to its understanding and practice. My resolution was then, and there, turned more positively toward the avenues of information, and I reached a determination, with a unanimity of all the forces of my mind, to ever throw the greatest possible light upon the subject, for the benefit of every honest and sincere seeker after its truth, who should follow in my footsteps. In the years that have elapsed since that time, I have ever held that experience in vivid recollection, and have sent no student away hungering or thirsting for information which it was in my power to impart; neither have I ever exacted or received in any instance, pecuniary compensation therefor.

Let it not be forgotten by the reader, that the author [James Wilson], in his time, was not a practitioner of astrology as a means of livelihood; hence was never able to make as broad and extensive an application of his observation as many others, whose necessities compelled them to constant and unremitting effort and experiment: thus he omitted to verify many aphorisms and truths of which others (perhaps less learned in general philosophy) had found abundant or convincing proof. I will be somewhat explicit in my statement of what appears to me to be erroneous in his enunciation of the cardinal principles of the ancient writers and commentators on the subject. The reader will observe that the author discards entirely the whole significance of the mansions or houses of the heavens, in the consideration of nativities; likewise the "essential dignity" of the planets; also the Moon's North and South Nodes; declaring, that as there is nothing except a point or place, no influence could possibly spring therefrom, unless it could come from nothing.

My own experience and observation have taught me that too much stress should not be placed upon the houses of the heavens, or predictions ventured based entirely upon the house in which a planet is posited, a transit occurs, or a direction falls; but I find a daily application of the usefulness of this division of the zodiac into mansions or houses.

Take, for example, the four angles of the figure, embracing the first, tenth, seventh and fourth houses of the heavens. Almost every person possessing any knowledge of a figure of the heavens, and competent to judge it, to any extent, has found experimental evidence of the fact that the angle of the east, or first house, ever exercises an influence over the personal affairs of the native, and fortunates or afflicts according to its strength or weakness. In the same manner it will be found that the angle of the south or tenth house influences the affairs of business, or profession, honors and reputation of the native; while the seventh house affects the concerns of wives, enemies, or opponents; and the fourth, or angle of the north, gives significance of real estate, of the ultimate of life, and in the language of the learned Mr. Lilly, "ever of the father of the native."

I have substantiated the truth of these in a general way, and with sufficient correspondence of detail to justify me in its promulgation as an astrological axiom. I have ever found in my practice, the Moon's Nodes significant in the character to which the ancient teachers have assigned them, viz: the North Node, benefic; and the South, malefic in influence. I am of the opinion that any person possessing a figure of the heavens for the time of their birth, can verify the truth of this ancient doctrine of the Nodes, by simply observing the time when the Sun, in its annual course through the zodiac, reaches the point or place of the South Node in the figure; for, at that time, annoyances, of greater or less degree, will ever mark the period, according to the directions, primary, and secondary, that are in force. This will enable the student in the science to offer some test of its truth to anyone whose nativity they may possess.

The principal lesson that the author has labored to inculcate, by the tenor of his comments, which I most heartily endorse, from whence every student may derive profit, is the wisdom of making general, rather than particular application of planetary influences. In other words, that it is more rational to give a good outline in any case than to attempt uncertain and imperfect detail.

In calculations involving so many and such varied qualities of influence, it is sufficient that a general classification of the forces is accomplished, and the student is never greater in modest self abnegation than when he has the grandeur of mind to say to the overcritical persons, with whom he comes in contact, who propound detailed questions, "I do not know."

In conclusion, permit me to say, that no grander or more soul-ennobling theme was ever presented to the human intellect, than the philosophy and language of the starry heavens. It opens to our inspection an endless volume of sublimated grandeur. It comprehends the incomputable in number; the immensity of space; the duration of eternity. Whoever, in the love of celestial mathematics, scans the vault of space, and by the aid of telescopic vision, searches for some new star or satellite, or watches fair Venus in her march across the solar disc, with nothing save the philosophy of distance, time, and motion, to subserve, will find a satisfaction beyond the more material consideration of mundane life; but unto him who reads the language of the heavens, and catches the inspiration of her loftier melodies, there is a charm, and enchantment, that makes every star a divinity, and lights all space with a prophetic vision.

Bibliography

Books

Adams, Evangeline. *Astrology for Everyone*. New York: Dodd, Mead & Co., 1931.
_____. *Astrology, Your Place Among the Stars*. New York: Dodd, Mead & Co., 1930.
_____. *Astrology, Your Place in the Sun*. New York: Dodd, Mead & Co., 1927.
_____. *The Bowl of Heaven*. New York: Dodd, Mead & Co., 1926.
_____. *The Bowl of Heaven*, with an Introduction by Lynn Wells. New York: Dodd, Mead & Co., 1970.
_____. *The Evangeline Adams Guide for 1933*, ed. George E. Jordan, Jr. New York: Dodd, Mead & Co., 1933.

Adams, Andrew N., ed. *A Genealogical History of Henry Adams of Braintree, Massachusetts and His Descendants*. Rutland, VT: The Tuttle Co, 1898. Reprinted by Parker River Researchers, Newburyport, MA, 1984.

Ashmand, J.M., translator. *Ptolemy's Tetrabiblos*. N. Hollywood, CA: Symbols & Signs, 1976.

Bankhead, Tallulah. *My Autobiography*. New York: Harper & Brothers, 1952.

Bennett, Ellen H. *Astrology, Science of Knowledge and Reason*. New York: Ellen H. Bennett, 1897.

Brau, Jean-Louis, Weaver, Helen and Edmonds, Allan. *Larousse Encyclopedia of Astrology*. New York: New American Library, 1982.

Brough, James. *Princess Alice*. Boston: Little, Brown & Co., 1975.

Broughton, Luke D., M.D. *Elements of Astrology*. New York: L.D. Broughton, 1898.

Brown, John Dennis. *101 Years on Wall Street, An Investor's Almanac*. Englewood Cliffs, NJ: Prentice Hall, 1991.

Burroughs, John. *Signs and Seasons*. New York: Harper & Row, 1981 (reprint of 1886 original).

Campion, Nicholas. *The Book of World Horoscopes*. Bristol, England: Cinnabar Books, 3rd printing revised, 1999.

Carter, Charles E.O. *An Introduction to Political Astrology*. London: L.N. Fowler & Co., 1951.

Cheiro (Louis Hamon). *Confessions: Memoirs of a Modern Seer*. London: Jarrods Publishers, 1932.
_____. *Cheiro's Memoirs: The Reminiscences of a Society Palmist*. London: William Rider and Son Ltd., 1912.
_____. *Palmistry for All*. New York: Prentice Hall Press, 1988 (reprint).

Christino, Karen. *Foreseeing the Future: Evangeline Adams and Astrology in America*. Amherst, MA: One Reed Publications, 2002.

Clemens, Marie Louise. *The Autobiography of Marie Louise Clemens*. Boston: Bruce Humphreys Publishers, 1953.

Coleman, Walter. *Astrology and the Law*. Greenlawn, NY: Casa de Capricornio Publishers, 1977.

Colville, W.J. *Our Places in the Universal Zodiac*. Sea Breeze, FL: Freedom Publishing Co., 1899.
_____. *Universal Spiritualism*. New York: R.F. Fenno & Co., 1906.

Cramer, Diane. *How to Give an Astrological Health Reading*. Tempe, AZ: American Federation of Astrologers, 1988.

Crowley, Aleister. *The Confessions of Aleister Crowley* ed. John Symonds and Kenneth Grant. London and NY: Arkana, 1969.

Crowley, Aleister and Adams, Evangeline. *The General Principles of Astrology* ed. Hymenaeus Beta. York Beach, ME: Redwheel/Weiser, 2002.

Culpeper, Nicholas. *Astrologicall Judgment of Diseases* London: Nath. Brookes, 1655 (Ballantrae reprint).

Curry, Patrick. *A Confusion of Prophets*. London: Collins & Brown, 1992.

Davis, Richard Harding. *Vera, the Medium*. New York: Chas. Scribner's Sons, 1908.

Dean, Geoffrey et al. *Recent Advances in Natal Astrology*. Bromley Kent, England: The Astrological Association, 1977.

Duncan, Isadora. *My Life*. New York: Boni & Liveright, Inc., 1927.

Felsenfeld, Carol. *Alice Roosevelt Longworth*. New York: St. Martin's Press, 1988.

Geist, Kenneth L. *The Life and Films of Joseph L. Mankiewicz*. New York: Charles Scribner's Sons, 1978.

Greenfield, Howard. *Caruso*. New York: G.P. Putnam's Sons, 1982.

Holden, James H. *A History of Horoscopic Astrology*. Tempe, AZ: American Federation of Astrologers, 1996.

Holden, James H. and Hughes, Robert A. *Astrological Pioneers of America*. Tempe, AZ: American Federation of Astrologers, 1988.

Kessler, Carol Farley. *Elizabeth Stuart Phelps*. Boston: Twayne Publishers, 1982.

Kirkpatrick, Sidney. *Edgar Cayce: An American Prophet*. New York: Riverhead Books, 2000.

Kurth, Paul. *Isadora: A Sensational Life*. Boston, New York and London: Little, Brown and Company, 2001.

Larsen, Stephen and Robin. *A Fire in the Mind, the Life of Joseph Campbell*. New York: Doubleday, 1991.

Lewi, Grant. *Astrology for the Millions*. St. Paul, MN: Llewellyn Publications, 1996.

Lilly, William. *Christian Astrology Books I and II*. London: Ascella Publications, 1999 (reprint of 1647 original).

Louis, Anthony. *Horary Astrology Plain and Simple*. St. Paul, MN: Llewellyn Publications, 1998.

MacDonald, J. Fred. *Don't Touch That Dial! Radio Programming in American Life*. Chicago: Nelson-Hall, 1979.

MacNeice, Louis. *Astrology*. Garden City, NY: Doubleday & Co., Inc., 1964.

McCaffery, Ellen. *Astrology, Its History and Influence in the Western World*. New York: Charles Scribner's Sons, 1942.
_____. "Horoscope of Evangeline Adams" in *The Best of the Illustrated National Astrological Journal*, ed. Edward A. Wagner. 1978.

Montgomery, Ruth. *Here and Hereafter*. New York: Ballantine Books, 1968.

Morris, Sylvia Jukes. *Edith Kermit Roosevelt*. New York: Coward, McCann & Geoghegan, Inc., 1980.

Omarr, Sydney. *My World of Astrology*. N. Hollywood, CA: Wilshire Book Co., 1965.

Phelps, Elizabeth Stuart. *Chapters from a Life*. New York: Houghton, Mifflin & Co., 1896.
_____. *The Gates Ajar*. Boston: Houghton, Mifflin & Co., 1868.
_____. *Men, Women and Ghosts*. New York: Garrett Press, Inc., 1969 (reprint of original stories published prior to 1869).
_____. *The Silent Partner*. Old Westbury, NY: The Feminist Press, 1983 (reprint of 1871 original).

Renehan, Edward J., Jr. *John Burroughs, An American Naturalist*. Post Mills, VT: Chelsea Green Publishing Co., 1992.

Rodden, Lois. *Astrodata III*. Tempe, AZ: American Federation of Astrologers, 1986.
_____. *Profiles of Women*. Tempe, AZ: American Federation of Astrologers, 1979.

Rose, Kenneth. *King George V*. London: Weidenfield & Nicholson, 1983.

Savage, Minot J., D.D. *The Passing and the Permanent in Religion*. New York and London: G.P. Putnam's Sons, 1901.

Scott, Michael. *The Great Caruso*. New York: Alfred A. Knopf, 1988.

Sheaffer, Louis. *O'Neill: Son and Artist*. Boston: Little, Brown and Co., 1973.

Smyth, Egbert Coffin. *In the Matter of the Complaint Against Egbert Coffin Smyth and Others*. Boston: Cupples, Upham & Co., 1887.

Spencer, Katherine Q. *The Zodiac Looks Westward*. Philadelphia and New York: David McKay Co., 1943.

Teal, Celeste. *Identifying Planetary Triggers*. St. Paul MN: Llewellyn Publications, 2000.

Thomas, Gordon and Morgan-Witts, Max. *The Day the Bubble Burst*. Garden City, NY: Doubleday & Co., 1979.

Tobey, Carl Payne. *Astrology of Inner Space*. Tucson, AZ: Omen Press, 1972.

Tyl, Noel. *Prediction in Astrology*. St. Paul, MN: Llewellyn Publications, 1991.

Watters, Barbara H. *Horary Astrology and the Judgment of Events*. Washington D.C.: Valhalla, 1973.

Wilson, James. *Dictionary of Astrology*. New York, NY: Samuel Weiser, Inc., 1971 (reprint of 1885 original).

Zoller, Robert. *Fate, Free Will and Astrology*. New York: Ixion Press, 1992.
_____. *Tools & Techniques of the Medieval Astrologers*. New York: Robert Zoller, 1981.

Magazines

Adams, Evangeline. "Find Birthdays in the Stars" *Pictorial Review*, October 1926.
_____. "Thirty Years of Star Gazing" *Woman's Home Companion*, June, 1925.

Campion, Nicholas. "Astrology, Politics and Ritual" *NCGR Journal*, Spring 1994.

Chaney, W.H. "The Astrologer's Vade Mecum" *The Sphinx* Volume II No. 1, February 1900.

Christino, Karen. "Evangeline Adams and the Airwaves" *Considerations* Vol. XIV #4, Winter '01-'02.

Grant, Madge. "Successful Personalities" for *American Club Women's Magazine*, reprinted in Adams' 1913 brochure.

Gray, Allison. "People Who Try to Get Tips from the Stars" *American Magazine*, December 1921.

Johnson, Alva. "Lady of the Stars" *New Yorker*, October 27, 1928.

Marsh, Daniel L. "All Noisy on the Medical Front" *Bostonia, The Boston University Alumni Magazine*, April 1940.

Morrison, Al H. "Testing a National Chart" *The Astrologers Newsletter*, October 1993.

Savage, Rev. M.J., "A Reply to Mr. Hawthorne" *The Arena*, Volume 3, 1889.

Smith, J. Heber, M.D. "Man in His Relation to the Solar System" *The Arena* Volume 15, December 1895.

Thompson, Catherine. "How to Give Judgment on the Sugar Map" *The Sphinx*, September 1899.
_____. "To the Editor" *Modern Astrology*, July-August, 1933.
_____. "An Illustrated Horoscope" *The Sphinx*, September to November 1899.

Newspaper Articles

Adams, Evangelina. "Horoscope of Greater New York" *New York Journal and Advertiser Sunday Supplement* April 30, 1899.

Albelli, Alfred. "Evangeline Adams Mate Involved in Love Theft" *New York News* December 31, 1931.

Engle, William. "Evangeline Adams in Death Joins the Prophets of the Ages" *NewYork World-Telegram* November 11, 1932.

Foster, Helen Herbert. "Seeks Wisdom Among the Stars" *Brooklyn Eagle Sunday Magazine* April 24, 1927.

Kuhn, Irene. "Astrologers Mate as Stars Dictated" *New York Herald* April 7, 1923.

Phelps, Mary. "What Happened When the Stars told a Wife What the Moon Saw" *New York Mirror* February 7, 1932.

Warton, Carl. "Predicts War in U.S. Within 15 Years" *The Boston Herald* April 27, 1930.

"Arriving Astrologist Sees New World War Due in 1942" Anon. *The Brooklyn Eagle* June 14, 1923.

"Believer in Stars Loses $100,000 Suit" Anon. *New York Times*, June 13, 1922.

"Beware of Market, for Hostile Uranus is in Control, Noted Astrologist Warns" Anon. *New York Telegram* February 4, 1930.

"Fire Destroys Windsor Hotel" Anon. *New York World* March 18, 1899.

"Foresees Industrial War" Anon. *New York Mail*, June 14, 1923.

"Foretold the Calamity" Anon. *New York World*, March 20, 1899.

"Joseph Jefferson Dangerously Ill" Anon. *New York Times*, April 14, 1905.

"Joseph Jefferson Dies at his Florida Home" Anon. *NY Times*, April 24, 1905.

"She is Astrologer, Not Fortune-Teller" Anon. *The World, NY*, December 12, 1914.

"Society Palmist Seized in a Raid" Anon. *The World, NY*, January 13, 1911.

"Stroke Fatal to Astrologer of Radio Fame" Anon. *New York American* November 11, 1932.

"Warren F. Leland Dead" Anon. *New York Times* April 5, 1899.

"Warren F. Leland Follows His Wife" Anon. *NY Journal-American* April 5, 1899.

"Warren Leland Prostrated by Shock" Anon. *NY Evening Journal* March 18, 1899.

Reference Works

A Thousand and One Notable Nativities Alan Leo's Astrological Manuals, No. 11. London: L.N. Fowler & Co. c. 1910.

Appleton's Cyclopaedia of American Biography. New York: D. Appleton & Co., 1886, 1888 (facsimile edition).

Astrodatabank CD Version 2.0. Manchester, MA: Astrodatabank Co., 2002.

Current Biography Yearbook. New York: H.W. Wilson Co., 1944, 1972, 1973.

Dictionary of American Biography. New York: James T. White & Co., 1936 and Charles Scribner's Sons, 1964.

Encyclopedia of Occultism and Parapsychology ed. Leslie Shepard. Detroit: Gale Research Co., 1984.

New York Criminal Reports, Volume XXXII, 1914 edition. Albany, NY: Charles N. Mills, W.C. Little & Co., 1915.

New York Historical Society Dictionary of Artists in America 1564-1880 ed. Grace C. Groce and David H. Wallace. New Haven, CT: Yale University Press, 1957.

Time Almanac 2000. Boston: Family Editing Co., 2001.

Who Was Who. Volume I-III London: Adam & Charles Black, 1967.

Who Was Who in American Art ed. Peter Hastings. Madison, CT: Sound View Press,1985.

Who Was Who in Journalism 1925-1928. Detroit MI: Gale Research Co. 1978.

Other Sources

Adams, Evangeline
    Sales brochures, "Scientific Astrology Explained" c. 1913 and "The Law and Astrology" c. 1915.
    Horoscope of Arthur Burroughs, Horoscope of Beatrice Jones, Horoscopes of Beatrice Cameron Mansfield and Richard Mansfield Jr.
    Letters to "Everybody": April 9, 1928, May 1, 1928, August 22, 1931.
    Letters to Lewis Mumford and Elonia C. Mumford July 1930.
    Letter to Gertrude November 3, 1932.

Dobin, Rabbi Joel C., Letter of November 11, 1994.

Winski, Norman,
    Evangeline Adams' library; scrapbook of Gertrude Adams Curry and Evangeline Adams Curry Elmore; interviews of October 9, 1993, June 4-5, 1994, and May 20, 2000.

Federal Census of 1900, 1910 and 1920.

National Climatic Data Center's *Data Time Series* from their *Global Historical Climatological Network, www.ncdc.noaa.gov.*

T.L. Bradford Scrapbooks at the Hahnemann University Library, Philadelphia, PA.

Various catalogs from the Boston University School of Medicine, 1897-1911.

Index